PRAISE FOR *THE CREATIVE PROCESS ILLUSTRATED*

"Here's what I love about this book: The authors ask really great questions, and they are clearly delighted with their hunt for the answers. This book will fuel many hours of discussion among students and professionals who are passionate about their creative work, and who seek thoughtful language, models, and guidance that support doing what they love to do."

—Wendy Richmond, author of *Art Without Compromise*
and columnist, *Communication Arts*

"This is a unique and engaging illustrated guide to the way some of the most brilliant creatives in advertising think, create and conceive ideas. Get into the minds of Kevin Roddy, Andy Azula, David Kennedy, or one of the other talented contributors. It's a fascinating and inspiring read; a must for anyone getting into the creative business of advertising."

—Kevin Swanepoel, President,
The One Club for Art & Copy, New York

"Finally someone has written a book that helps me figure out what the hell's been happening in my brain for the past fifteen years! Inside you'll find a smart dissection of the creative process and how it's applied. You'll get to see how some of today's top creative minds work. Each of them has illustrated their individual idea processes. It's as if they've tipped their brains out on the page and we're all allowed to go explore."

—Lucy Collier, Creative Director,
Platform - Wieden+Kennedy, London

"Glenn Griffin and Deborah Morrison have ventured where few others have gone before— deep into the minds and thought processes of some of advertising's most brilliant creators. The result is enlightening and inspiring for anyone who cares about creative thinking, idea generation, and the quest for originality. The drawings alone are priceless!"

—Warren Berger, author of *Advertising Today* and *Glimmer:
How Design Can Transform Your Life and Maybe Even the World*

D1127301

"A book about creativity that's also creative. Seeing how creative minds work made mine work just a little better. This remarkable collection of drawings reveals so much about how ideas come to life, it's sure to get you thinking about how you think. Could there be a better reason to buy this book?"

—Brett Robbs, Ph.D., Associate Professor,
University of Colorado, Boulder

"A fantastic book for all those who fear the empty white page."

—Ignacio Oreamuno, President, IHAVEANIDEA

"Using the advertising industry as the focal point and vehicle for exploration, *The Creative Process Illustrated* spans a wide and diverse spectrum of disciplines— from social psychology to photography to behavioral science—that together paint a complete picture of the cultural landscape which the creative process inhabits."

—Maria Popova, Planner, TBWA\Chiat\Day
(Los Angeles) and editor, Brain Pickings
(www.brainpickings.org)

"There's the science of creativity and there's the muse of it, and *The Creative Process Illustrated* nails them both. This is a fantastic read for anyone who wants to peek inside the brains of people who do some of the best advertising in the world. Now, if it had only been written two years ago, maybe I'd still have a job."

—Erik Proulx, founder of Please Feed The Animals and
creator of the documentary *Lemonade*

"Wow... a remarkable study of creative conceptualization that taps some of the greatest creative minds in advertising. This book unlocks many creative secrets and opens new areas of inquiry into advertising creativity."

—Tom Reichert, Ph.D., Professor, University of Georgia and
author of *Erotic History of Advertising*

"This book offers new insight into the theory and practice of the creative process in advertising, and will advance efforts to prepare students to become better creative thinkers and problem solvers."

—Thomas Vogel, Ph.D., Associate Professor, Emerson College, Boston

THE CREATIVE PROCESS

ILLUSTRATED

(how advertising's big ideas are born)

W. GLENN GRIFFIN AND DEBORAH MORRISON

HOW BOOKS
Cincinnati, Ohio
WWW.HOWDESIGN.COM

THE CREATIVE PROCESS ILLUSTRATED. Copyright © 2010 by W. Glenn Griffin and Deborah Morrison. Manufactured in China. All rights reserved. No other part of this book may be reproduced in any form or by any electronic or mechanical means including information storage and retrieval systems without permission in writing from the publisher, except by a reviewer, who may quote brief passages in a review.
Published by HOW Books, an imprint of F+W Media, Inc., 4700 East Galbraith Road, Cincinnati, Ohio 45236. (800) 289-0963. First edition.

For more excellent books and resources for designers, visit www.howdesign.com.

14 13 12 11   5 4 3 2

Distributed in Canada by Fraser Direct
100 Armstrong Avenue
Georgetown, Ontario, Canada L7G 5S4
Tel: (905) 877-4411

Distributed in the U.K. and Europe by David & Charles
Brunel House, Newton Abbot, Devon, TQ12 4PU, England
Tel: (+44) 1626-323200, Fax: (+44) 1626-323319
E-mail: postmaster@davidandcharles.co.uk

Distributed in Australia by Capricorn Link
P.O. Box 704, Windsor, NSW 2756 Australia
Tel: (02) 4577-3555

Library of Congress Cataloging-in-Publication Data

Griffin, W. Glenn.
  The creative process illustrated / W. Glenn Griffin and Deborah Morrison.
    p. cm.
  ISBN 978-1-60061-960-1 (pbk. : alk. paper)
  1. Advertising. 2. Creative ability in business. I. Morrison, Deborah. II. Title.
  HF5823.G723 2010
  659.1--dc22
                          2010012984

Edited by AMY SCHELL OWEN
Designed by GRACE RING
Production coordinated by GREG NOCK

DEDICATION

Mom and Dad, Ginger, Sabrina and Audrey Ann: You're what it's all about.
Deborah, my mentor and friend: You'll never know the difference you make.

—W. Glenn Griffin

First, as always, to Dan and the wild boyz, who lift my spirit and inspire me.
You guys are amazing.

Second, to Glenn, who could be the brightest and funniest guy in the world.
You make me smarter, and I appreciate that.

—Deborah Morrison

ACKNOWLEDGMENTS

The smart, generous and fascinatingly creative people who contributed their work
to this project are our heroes. Thank you for your patience with all the e-mails, faxes
and legal forms. But most of all, thanks for raising the bar. This book celebrates you.

To Amy Schell Owen, editor extraordinaire, we say thanks for your patience, advice
and tremendous expertise from day one. We'd also like to thank Megan Patrick for
recognizing the merit in our book proposal and Grace Ring for the beautiful design
work. The team at HOW Books is terrific.

The following people also pitched in to help us with this project in unique and
wonderful ways. To each of them, we owe a debt of gratitude.

Chris Adams	Jen Larkin Kuzler
Mark Allen	Lisa Langford
Patty Alvey	Erin Larsen
Warren Berger	Hilary Lee
José Bowen	Matthew Lindner
Anne Bev Branch	Suzanne Lucas
Richard Campos	Ben Malbon
JoEllyn Carrel	Dan Morrison
Meme Drumwright	Ignacio Oreamuno
Amy Feezor	Cathy Ormerod
Tim Gleason	Sandy Parkerson
Holly Grayson	Marina Pietracci
Jonas Greene	Maria Popova
Debbie Harvey	Rahul Pula
Karen Howle	Kim Sheehan
Mark Huslig	Greg Warden

ABOUT THE AUTHORS

 **W. GLENN GRIFFIN, PH.D.**, teaches courses in creativity and portfolio development and leads the Method Creative program at SMU's Temerlin Advertising Institute in Dallas, Texas. His research on creativity, education and social responsibility has appeared in the *Journal of Advertising*, the *Journal of Advertising Education* and *Journalism and Mass Communication Educator*, among other publications. His students' work has been featured in both national and international press, including *Advertising Age*, *Adweek* and *CMYK* magazines and recognized by The One Club for Art & Copy, the Art Directors Club of New York and the Clio Awards, among many other organizations. He is a frequent speaker at professional and academic conferences on the topics of creativity, advertising education and social responsibility. He lives in Richardson, Texas, but will always call his native Tuscaloosa, Alabama, "home." Photo ©2009 Jim Herndon www.onlocationportraiture.com.

 **DEBORAH MORRISON, PH.D.**, is the Chambers Distinguished Professor of Advertising at the University of Oregon. For two decades (maybe a little more), she's worked with students in Oregon and at the University of Texas at Austin, where she built Texas Creative, one of the best university-based portfolio programs in the country. At the University of Oregon, she and her colleagues developed the successful creative strategist model, wherein all advertising specialties are grounded in creativity and strategic thinking. Morrison served on The One Club for Art & Copy's board of directors for two terms (and is the only university educator to do so). She's judged regional, national and international shows for students and professionals. She's honored to have won the University of Oregon School of Journalism and Communication's Jonathan Marshall Award for Innovative Teaching in 2008 and 2009 (the only two-time winner). She was awarded the William Blunk Professorship for teaching at the University of Texas and recognized as an ADC GrandMaster in education by the Art Directors Club in New York. She is also a founding patron of Platform, the Wieden+Kennedy creative lab in London. With Brett Robbs, she co-authored the book *Idea Industry: How to Crack the Advertising Career Code*. She's had the good fortune of visiting, studying and thinking about hundreds of agencies while learning from thousands of students, to whom she owes so much. She lives in Eugene, Oregon, with her dashing photojournalist husband Dan, and three wonderful sons, all of whom are growing up to be astounding men.

TABLE OF
CONTENTS

FOREWORD

No one knows, exactly, when a baby will be born.

We can estimate a due date. We can peer in and predict, we can measure this and monitor that. Yet for all our technological devices and medical advances, birth is still very much the domain of art, not science. We don't decide when babies will be born. Babies do.

Ideas, like babies, decide when to be born. They defy prediction.

Just as we can't predict which jokes will make us laugh, or which person will spin us madly in love, the creative process isn't really a "process" at all. Yes, we can dissect every step someone goes through to develop a creative idea, but at some point there's a quantum leap from A to B to C to K. How does it work? Where does it start? When will it happen?

The reality is, creativity simply isn't rational. It's sweaty and red-blooded. Tempestuous. It wakes up at 2 A.M. struggling whether to tweak a headline one hundredth of an inch, or start over entirely.

When I began in advertising, the creative process seemed almost supernatural. How could anyone possibly distill the intricacies of a brand, then hone them into an idea sharp enough to cut through people's natural resistance, into their hearts and their brains, ultimately connecting with the magical decision-making hot button that decides which toothpaste or hotel room or politician to choose? I had no idea how a plain, dull fact could metamorphosize into an idea with the power to change behaviors and beliefs.

It seemed like alchemy, transforming a lump of raw information into the golden idea.

Since then, I've learned that the creative process really is alchemy. Very much so. Creative people defend the world from predictability, one idea at a time. They don't just write and design and art direct—they articulate our most personal unspoken insecurities and intentions. They don't just sell— they show us what matters.

And that's why, geeky though it may be, I love the whole sloppy mess of creativity in my work. I love when a brand needs to figure out who it is, what it stands for, why people should care. I love working with smart creative people, developing thoughts that leave the world an ever so slightly more interesting place than before those thoughts were thought.

The process of creativity is especially important today—in any industry, and any discipline, at any level. Because for all its maddening imprecision, creativity always triumphs. Information comes and goes. Transactions can be outsourced. Technology becomes obsolete. Opinions change, and tastes change even faster. But creativity will always be essential, and rare.

Creativity is the difference between information and genius. It's the difference between transcribing a dictionary and writing. When you see people in awe of Google's algorithm or Apple's devices, remember: The ultimate technology is you.

One day, at a low point in my own career, while riding in a taxi through San Francisco, I saw a graffiti sentence spray-painted in 10-foot tall letters. "I just feel like something wonderful is about to happen." That sentence changed my life. Why? Something wonderful is always about happen, if you're ready. If you understand that creativity, like life, is a process. You can't know what comes next, because like babies and tears and falling in love, creativity is gloriously imperfect.

That's where this book comes in. We get to stroll around as guests in the brains of the smartest thinkers, learning exactly how their ideas are born. Read, savor, ponder, and then ask yourself a question: In your own life, what extraordinary thing will you create that's irrepressibly, inimitably, audaciously you?

—**Sally Hogshead**, speaker, brand innovation consultant, and author of *Fascinate: Your 7 Triggers to Persuasion and Captivation*, and *Radical Careering: 100 Truths to Jumpstart Your Job, Your Career, and Your Life*

INTRODUCTION

"The difference between the forgettable and the enduring is artistry."

—Bill Bernbach, Co-Founder of Doyle Dane Bernbach (DDB), 1911–1982

Creativity, that enigmatic force, is the foundation upon which the advertising business is built. It's the precious commodity that agencies offer their clients. Product benefits, unique selling propositions, brand extensions: All those factors, all those buzzwords don't mean anything to real people. But the right creative strategy can make them accessible and relevant to their lives.

In advertising, creative directors, art directors and writers are the translators. They find ways to make soda sing. They make deodorant sexy. They convince us that we'll never be our best without the right running shoe. If you think about it, these ad folks are astoundingly good at what they do. They help us make decisions, form opinions and develop habits with a level of skill and authority commonly associated with parents, priests or police officers. Let's be honest: We'd rather hear "Just do it" from Nike.

Advertising, at its best, can be artful. It can be smart, educational and responsible—a wonder to behold. People in this business are masterful problem solvers. Their ideas can be potent. ("Yes we can!") Their work can shape culture. ("Whassup?") It's not hard to see why some of the brightest minds in the world are attracted to this industry.

As professors of advertising, we've had the privilege of working with brilliant young people on a daily basis, and we're constantly amazed by their optimism, energy and capacity for innovation. Year after year, our students win prestigious awards, display their work in elite exhibitions and continue to re-imagine the role that advertising can play in society. Alums are working for agencies around the world. We're watching them raise the bar, armed with the conviction that great ideas are powerful and transformative.

But how do great ideas happen?

As mentors to aspiring art directors and writers, we spend a lot of time helping people understand how to develop and leverage their natural creative ability. We know that the ability to think creatively is something innate; our students have decided to channel it into a career. They come to us with an agenda: Help me figure out how my brain works and how I can use it better to do something I love. The journey will be unique for each student, because no two brains are exactly alike. Each brings a different rhythm, perspective and personality to the exercise. We offer tools and feedback. We offer advice. We talk people off the ledge in the wake of failure. We celebrate triumphs! And all along the way, we never cease to be amazed by the beauty and diversity of each individual's creative process. That's the delicious spot where we live as teachers. Yes, it's important to build a smart portfolio of work as a credential for employment. We help kids do that. But from our perspective (and inevitably one day, our students'), understanding one's own mind and how it can be most creatively productive is truly the gift that keeps on giving.

The creative process is bigger than a profession. It's transcendent. People who truly understand and embrace their creative ability live fuller, happier lives. And the fact that a lot of them work in advertising shouldn't surprise anyone. We'd argue it's one of the most enjoyable ways to spend an eighty-hour workweek.

As you might expect, we're a couple of advertising junkies. We thrive upon listening to, reading, watching, clicking, experiencing and (sorry, Mr. Whipple) squeezing it. Did you see those gorgeous watercolor illustrations in the ads for Bell Canoes? The music in the Target commercials just makes us happy. How do they keep turning dog food into poetry for Pedigree? It can be a lovefest. We can get mushy.

Of course, we're also passionate enough to get angry when we see ugly stuff (sadly, there's so much of it out there). Yes, we've written letters. We've thrown fits in class and told our students, "Don't you ever do that!"

But loving advertising, like loving anything or anyone, means believing in how good it can be and always hoping the best expectations will be fulfilled. For our part, we've always wished that the world could understand and appreciate more of the humanity that's invested in the ads they love. We know the people behind the best work that our industry has to offer (many of them personally, the rest of them spiritually), and we consider them heroes. And in a business that takes (and, let's face it, sometimes earns) a lot of criticism, perhaps it's time for a fresh perspective.

It's time to think about thinking. It's time to appreciate the development of advertising as a fascinatingly interesting intellectual pursuit. It's time to see the faces and hear the stories of men and women who could've done any number of meaningful things with their lives, but chose to do this (and to do it so well!). This book is a tribute to their professionalism, their achievements and their struggles. It's also a wonderful testimony to the unique and wonderful brain each of them uses to earn a living. It will, we hope, inspire more smart, optimistic and ambitious people to follow in their footsteps.

Most importantly, we'd like for this book to serve as documentation that creative directors, art directors and writers in advertising are some of the great artists and thinkers of our time. Considering the scope and power of their influence in our culture, that's not such a crazy idea.

—W. Glenn Griffin and Deborah Morrison

CHAPTER ONE
PROCESS IS PURE

Most people, when they see an ad, never think about how it came to be. In fact, people don't consciously engage with most advertising, period. It's noise. It's part of the landscape. It blends in. And for the same reason you're unlikely to notice any particular tree during a walk through a neighborhood park, you probably won't pay any attention to a television commercial, billboard, radio spot, web banner or any other branded message unless it's different in some significant way. We've convinced ourselves that we've seen everything before. That makes advertising a very tough business.

Those great ads that do break through—the very best of the lot—are those that do the job for the client (they communicate about the product and satisfy strategic objectives) and also leave consumers happier, wiser... somehow better for having engaged with the ad (they deliver a "gift" in exchange for their attention). When an ad sells and does so with great style, it's a thing of beauty. But when ads simply do one or the other, they fall short of fulfilling their potential. The creative folks that make ads every day strive to find the right balance of the two.

Advertising is a thoroughly collaborative business. Inside ad agencies, teams of professionals who specialize in marketing, research, media, technology, production and creativity (the list can go on, depending on the project) work together to serve the client's needs. It makes sense, then, that just about every ad you see that's selling a big brand is the end product

of mammoth interaction—the sum of many edits, revisions, restarts and critiques by many different people. Everyone's got fingerprints on the work.

Within that collaborative machine, creative directors supervise the art directors (the visual people) and writers (the word people) working on a specific account. Typically, one art director and one writer are paired to work together to generate ideas, but creative teams can vary in size (and sometimes specialty) if need be. The creative directors are the more senior and experienced pros who started out in art direction or writing. These days, they guide the work of their own teams, assuring that it meets the agency's standards and (with any luck) the client's, too. The creative ideas they generate get circulated throughout the agency; those determined to be the strongest are shared with the client. The client's evaluation of the work can send it back for revision, push it through to see the light of day as a finished ad or kill it in favor of another approach. (That's a woefully simple summary of how things can happen, but you get the idea.) A great idea can run that gauntlet, but it can seem miraculous whenever it happens.

At the center of all this (and, regrettably, too often overlooked) are the individuals who've invested their big brains in this enterprise. They might have been geneticists or screenwriters or architects or economists or poet laureates, but they chose to make advertising. They'll tell you they do it because they love it, and because they couldn't imagine being happier doing something else. They're creative people, yes... but of a rare breed. They don't create as a means of pure self-expression. Instead, they enjoy the challenge of doing something imaginative/surprising/amazing/smart/beautiful that will meet someone else's specifications and solve their problems. They don't sign their works of art. They labor in anonymity. Think about it: In this business, a writer can pen a phrase on every American's lips ("Can you hear me now?") but only his mom gives him credit. An art director's colorful vision of dancing silhouettes enjoying the iPod is more ubiquitous than Warhol, but museum curators don't know her name.

We're fascinated by the creative minds that answer the call to be professional creatives. These individuals are at the core of everything that makes advertising interesting. They are true artists in the sense that their work is constantly broadening, enriching and challenging our concept of that term. Each of them brings a unique intellectual perspective to the work they do, and their talent is a hot commodity. Agencies (the good ones, anyway) understand that they have to recruit the best brains available. After all, their piece of a 500 billion dollar industry is at stake.

For that reason, these creatives understand more about their own brains than most of us do. Working in this business, they've honed their own creative process for developing ideas. That personal process, we believe, is representative of advertising creativity in its purest form.

feels very big, and it's often used to describe anything that's new, different, odd or unexpected. Even though it's easy to carelessly throw the term around, "creative" also carries connotations of something special, rare or valuable. It seems intuitive, therefore, that the true definition of the word must be somewhere in the middle.

To complicate matters further, for centuries now, creativity has also been attached to the magical or supernatural. It's been the topic of much romance and fantasy. The classical Greek philosopher Plato (c. 427–c. 347 B.C.) explained that goddesses known as the Muses inspired mankind's artistic creations,

---

Creative directors, art directors and writers see the mind as an instrument. It's the most important tool they use at work.

Creativity is advertising's most valuable resource. Studying, understanding and appreciating the nature of the creative process, we believe, should be a priority in the scholarly realm; this area of inquiry holds the potential to accentuate advertising's significant contributions to culture and quality of life.

Remarkably, the study of creativity and the creative process is still rather new. This chapter will offer you an overview of research, definitions for some important terms, theoretical insights and a sense of how advertising connects to it all.

WHAT IS CREATIVITY?

In order to study something, it's essential to start with a definition that precisely describes the topic of interest and distinguishes it from others. Historically, that's been one of the major obstacles to the study of creativity. The term "creative"

attributing no innate creative agency/ability to human beings. Hundreds of years later, the poet Alexander Pope (1688–1744) was celebrating his own Muse and Rudyard Kipling (1865–1936), author of *The Jungle Book*, cited a "daemon" that lived in his pen, perpetuating the link between creative works and otherworldly forces.

Over the past century, scholarly research on creativity was confounded by a number of issues. First, and perhaps most significantly, creative thinking isn't a readily observable phenomenon. While we might be able to see ideas or other creative products realized, trying to figure out how or where they originated in the human mind is a different story. So far, science hasn't developed a viable method for watching us think in real time and certainly not at a level of sophistication that can differentiate creative thinking from any other type.

Second, creativity was long considered a peripheral psychological phenomenon, meaning that most experts viewed creative thinking as either a secondary (less significant) cognitive function or one that wasn't commonly experienced by most people. And, as we've already noted, the lack of a clear and concise definition of creativity was a great obstacle in getting studies off the ground.

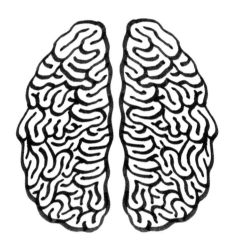

Creativity as Problem Solving

Despite the fact that the study of creativity remains relatively new, a more rational, focused and practical view of it has begun to emerge. The most widely accepted scholarly definition of the term now frames it as a problem-solving activity. However, not every solution to a problem is necessarily a creative solution.

Harvard University professor Teresa Amabile, in her book *The Social Psychology of Creativity*, identifies two types of solutions: (a) *algorithmic solutions* (preexisting, linear series of steps to be followed); and (b) *heuristic solutions* (new methods developed in the absence of algorithms). Clearly, a "creative" solution would be considered heuristic in nature rather than algorithmic, because it represents a new approach for solving a problem.

In advertising, the challenge to solve a client's problems is ever present. How can people be convinced to drink more milk? What can be said about tires that hasn't already been said? Is there a way to position this personal computer as the hip, youthful alternative to the market leader? Algorithms abound. Formulaic approaches (those tried-and-true templates that clients love) are everywhere. The best art directors and writers will look for a new (heuristic) approach for crafting brand messages in a crowded, copycat category.

Novelty

Novelty, in fact, is another essential element in defining creativity. Case in point: Scholars in the field of aesthetics argue that novelty is a key characteristic for evaluating works of art. Experimental research evidence suggests that creatively productive people prefer novelty, attributable to a characteristic open-mindedness and distaste for the traditional or commonplace in everyday life. It is important to note, however, that the "new" or "novel" can be derived from the old; the creative mind can combine or synthesize existing material to yield new products. Some may suggest that "there's nothing new under the sun," but creativity defies this perspective by discovering new combinations, connections and relationships.

Agency creatives live in constant fear of becoming hacks. There's great pressure to avoid ripping off (whether by accident or on purpose) someone else's work or producing something that is boring and flat. Of course, it can be hard to discern whether or not an idea for an ad is original when you're so immersed in the business. Luke Sullivan, group creative director at the agency GSD&M and the author of *Hey Whipple, Squeeze This: A Guide to Creating Great Ads*, suggests that art directors and writers should admire good work that others do but then promptly forget it. Perhaps easier said than done, but wise words nonetheless.

Usefulness

If we think of creativity as a method of problem solving, it's easy to understand how the creativity of an idea could be measured by how useful it is. If we solve a problem, the method used for solving it was beneficial to us. This also introduces the idea that creativity makes a valuable contribution (at some level) in people's lives and isn't purely self-serving. There's a sense that creativity has an inherent social value. Arthur J. Cropley, emeritus professor of psychology at the University of Hamburg, insists that creative ideas must be shared and "accepted or at least tolerated" by society, which he calls "sociocultural validation."

No matter how "creative" we might consider an ad or a campaign to be from a variety of other perspectives, its ability to fulfill the client's objectives is key. Many industry award shows reward agencies for producing work that's funny or beautiful or represents a unique approach. However, if the advertising isn't doing the job for the client, it's unlikely to remain visible long enough to have a lasting cultural impact.

Everyone is creative.
And by that, we mean everyone has the potential to be.

Creativity Defined

The definition of creativity that we like to use encompasses all of the important criteria that we've outlined below.

> **Creativity:** The generation, development and transformation of ideas that are both novel and useful for solving problems.

Notice that we frame ideas as the product of creativity. We find that this resonates with our advertising students, whose credentials as "idea people" will be crucial to their success in the classroom and beyond.

For ad professionals, this definition probably reads a bit like a job description. As you'll hear many of them say, "You're only as good as your last idea."

But hey, no pressure.

WHO IS CREATIVE?

Ask a simple question, get a simple answer. Everyone is creative. And by that, we mean everyone has the potential to be. Potential is a key word.

In the *Handbook of Creativity*, cognitive psychologists Thomas B. Ward, Steven M. Smith and Ronald A. Finke insist "the capacity for creative thought is the rule rather than the exception in human cognitive functioning."

That's a pretty powerful statement. Read it again. It means that every normal, healthy human being on the planet is born ready to be creative. But note the word "capacity" there. That's where potential figures in. Creativity is, we believe, an act of will. If you want to think creatively, you can. If you want to be more creative than you are now, you can be that, too. But if you don't believe that you're creative or (worse yet) don't want to try it, don't expect anything much to change.

We try to help students believe in their own creative ability by framing it as good old-fashioned hard work. It's not magic (even though some of advertising's rock stars make it seem so). Hours of thinking, sketching, writing and rewriting will pay dividends. Quality ideas come from great quantities of ideas. Amazing creative work doesn't come easy, but that wonderful sense of accomplishment in finding the answer makes it all worthwhile. These are our mantras.

We encourage students to figure out how they are most creatively productive on a personal level. We don't make anyone creative; we help facilitate their journey. Finding your own process comes from a lot of trial and error (and let's be real here, there's lots and lots of error involved). Each student will experiment with different thinking techniques, a variety of work environments and all sorts of idiosyncratic philosophies and motivations. But eventually, things will start to click. As they taste success, they'll begin to trust the protocols they've developed. They'll settle into patterns that feel comfortable and yield the best results. Watching this happen is one of the best parts of our job.

Although no two people find ideas in exactly the same way, it's pretty clear that some aspects of the process are universal. In the next section, we'll offer an overview of research on the creative process and some related concepts.

THE CREATIVE PROCESS

It seems oddly appropriate that the most significant theory about how the creative process works came from an unlikely source. Graham Wallas (1858–1932), a British political scientist and sociologist, proposed one of the first significant models of the creative process in his book, *The Art of Thought* (1926). Although he spent most of his life teaching and writing about politics, he was fascinated by human nature and how it influenced the development of society.

Graham Wallas (1858–1932)

It seems oddly appropriate that the most significant theory about how the creative process works came from an unlikely source.

The Four-Stage Process Model

Wallas believed the creative process could be described as a series of four stages:

Preparation: The problem to be solved is carefully considered and resources are gathered in order to confront the task. The conscious mind is focused on the problem.

Incubation: Drawing upon these resources, consideration of the problem is internalized and becomes a largely subconscious activity. The mind makes connections more freely and abundantly.

Illumination: Possible solutions to the problem transition from subconscious to conscious thought. This is a moment of insight and optimism.

Verification: Solutions are tested and may be applied if shown to be viable.

Inherent to Wallas's model are several important assumptions. First, his conceptualization of the process makes it seem relatively simple. This was counterintuitive for many people back in 1926 and remains controversial in some circles today. In response, we'd argue that Wallas's four stages represent the more universally experienced facets of process but don't prohibit examination of the phenomenon in greater depth. Preparation, incubation, illumination and verification are also described as sequential, discrete stages. Wallas believed that they are experienced in the order presented and don't overlap. However, he did propose that the creative process is recursive in nature, meaning that any of its stages can be revisited, if necessary, once they've been completed in their original sequence. For example, if solutions tested at the verification stage are not shown to be viable for solving the problem, an

individual might decide to continue thinking (return to incubation) or start all over again from scratch (restart at preparation).

Not only does the Four-Stage Process Model resonate with advertising students, it also parallels the day-to-day work of ad professionals as well. In the agency setting, creative teams typically receive documents called *creative briefs* at the start of work on a new project. The creative brief (if well written) offers a summary of important research that then kick-starts that creative process. It also articulates the big problem(s) that advertising needs to solve for the client. Art directors and writers spend a lot of their time "incubating" about problems before discussing ideas with their partners and identifying the best possible solutions. Creative directors then consider this work and offer their advice and input. A few sound concepts are eventually presented to the client, where the ultimate verification moment happens. Based on that verdict, the creative team will know whether it's time to move ahead with production of the work or to go back to the drawing board. Thank goodness it's a recursive process, right?

More than eighty years later, Wallas's model is still the most famous and influential proposal for understanding how creative thinking unfolds as a process. The vast majority of models offered by other scholars bear a strong resemblance to Wallas's work. Hungarian mathematician George Pólya (1887–1985) proposed a model of the creative process that included a period of post-verification analysis (he called it "looking back"). Philosopher John Dewey's (1859–1952) book, *How We Think: A Restatement of the Relation of Reflective Thinking to the Educative Process* (1933), described a problem-solving process of "reflective thinking," including a "pre-reflective" phase that closely parallels Wallas's preparation and incubation stages. The powerful influence of the Four-Stage Process Model is well documented and persistent. The terms preparation, incubation, illumination and verification have become well known and widely accepted in both scholarly and professional contexts.

In 1944, advertising executive James Webb Young (1886–1973) acknowledged Graham Wallas in the introduction to his book *A Technique for Producing Ideas*, noting that "[Wallas] arrives at somewhat the same conclusions" about the creative process but that "what follows has seemed to have a particular usefulness for workers in advertising." Webb's explanation for how advertising ideas are generated was indeed

(1) **preparation**
(2) **incubation**
(3) **illumination**
(4) **verification**

reminiscent of Wallas's model, but Webb insisted that he "discovered" Wallas after developing his own theories.

The Structure of Intellect Model

Another important contribution to our understanding of how the mind works (and thinks creatively) is the Structure of Intellect (SI) model created by J.P. Guilford in 1967. Guilford, a psychologist, appreciated the interdependent relationship between human intelligence (the sum of a person's knowledge) and intellect (a person's ability to use knowledge and generate new ideas). The Structure of Intellect proposes that there are three dimensions of intellectual abilities:

Contents: The sum of our knowledge (our intelligence)—everything that we know and the various types of information represented there.

Operations: How we use knowledge—the various types of manipulations that we bring to bear upon our intelligence.

Products: New knowledge or ideas that are the results of thinking.

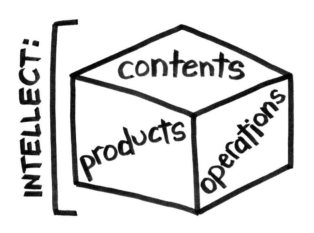

The "operations" referenced in SI include "thinking strategies" which can be learned and practiced, providing more evidence that people can develop their creative ability if they are motivated to do so. Most of the advertising creatives we know have their own favorite techniques for finding ideas. For example, some are list makers (e.g., lists of product characteristics, lists of alternative uses for a product, lists of places where the product could be used), and others enjoy sketching *mind maps* (a terrific divergent thinking tool developed in the 1960s). We share these techniques (and

RING bracelet
finger earring
wedding phone
engagement clang
guard circle
signet gang
nose eternity
key surround
napkin encircle

many others) with our students. With experience, each person decides which of these thinking tools work best or might be most useful in certain situations. They lend a bit of structure to process and help reduce some of the anxiety presented by a blank page.

An example of a mind map.

Essentially, SI helps us to understand intellect as a broader, richer concept encompassing how we think and how we leverage our intelligence in doing so. Guilford's work serves to augment our understanding of the processes associated with creative thought and complements the broader framework represented by Wallas's model.

Domains of Creativity

Creativity isn't limited to the fine and performing arts, of course. It manifests itself in just about everything human beings make or do. It's part of groundbreaking mathematical formulas, site plans for urban gardening and every seasonal vaccine against the flu. Although the theories and models we've discussed so far describe how the creative process works in general, a growing number of scholars believe that creative thinking may happen in different ways across the variety of contexts in which it is applied. This idea is called *domain specificity*. The term "domain" can refer to a body of knowledge or, better suited to our discussion, a particular profession or line of work. In his book, *Creativity: Flow and the Psychology of Discovery and Invention*, psychology professor Mihaly Csikszentmihalyi calls domains "primarily ways to make a living," adding that they are possibly "the best evidence of human creativity" because we built them ourselves.

If you think about it, it does seem intuitive that the creative process a choreographer uses to develop a new routine might follow different protocols than those an art director/writer team might use to develop an ad campaign. However, it's also a safe bet that both choreographers and advertising pros engage in preparation, incubation, illumination and verification as part of the work that they do. So, accepting the idea that the creative process might be adaptable to a particular

We don't know much at all about how the ideas behind great campaigns are developed or how the minds of art directors and writers find them.

domain shouldn't invalidate the more general models of the creative process. Instead, this capacity speaks to the great problem-solving nature of creativity itself.

Advertising is a domain, as are dance, architecture, chemistry and engineering. Domain specificity suggests there's a creative process signature to every business. Certainly, we see it in ad agencies (on a macro level) as clients, account planners, creative teams and other parties interact and follow established protocols to get the work done. More specifically, we can also observe processes for writing creative briefs and preparing pitches. We don't know much at all, however, about how the ideas behind great campaigns are developed or how the minds of art directors and writers find them. It appears we have more work to do.

Putting the Creative Process to Work

If you're a creative thinker, you use your mind in ways that everyone can, but too few actually do. You like solving problems. You embrace challenges. You use your creative ability in every aspect of your life, at work and at home.

We've discussed the idea that the creative process is universal in the sense that there are stages we all experience. We all draw upon our intelligence as the raw material for developing new ideas via the intellect.

However, we apply the creative process in a variety of different settings to accomplish a variety of different tasks. Consider the daily life of an executive chef. She spends her days running a kitchen, hiring staff, monitoring costs, rewriting menus and overseeing the operations of the restaurant. She might even prepare some food now and then. Each of these responsibilities requires special expertise and each presents its share of problems to be solved. Broadly speaking, cooking is the executive chef's domain and she uses her creative ability to perform in that context. But she's not always at work, of course. At home, she enjoys gardening and is looking for a space to plant fresh herbs. She's trying to figure out the best way to tutor her daughter in algebra. And her husband wants her help arranging the furniture in his new office. Hmmm. Our executive chef finds all sorts of applications for her creative problem-solving skills.

Creativity-Relevant Processes and Domain-Relevant Skills

Creative thinkers adapt their skills to address whatever problem is at hand. According to Harvard professor Teresa Amabile, these can be broadly categorized as creativity-relevant processes and domain-relevant skills.

Creativity-relevant processes incorporate more intuitive and generally applicable ways of thinking that help us generate exceptional (read: more creative) solutions.

Here are some examples of creativity-relevant processes:

- looking for solutions that aren't as obvious to others
- throwing out old strategies and pursuing new directions
- appreciating and being comfortable with complexity
- appreciating and being comfortable with ambiguity
- refusing to prematurely pass judgment on ideas

Amabile proposes that those who possess these abilities will find use for them regardless of the domain in which they are applied.

Alternatively, *domain-relevant skills* are also essential for creative thinking but are not used in every context. Instead, they are applied when we are solving problems in our particular line of work. For example, knowing how to simplify an equation is an essential skill for anyone tutoring students in algebra. It's valuable in that particular domain. However, that skill likely wouldn't be as valuable when writing poetry. Domain-relevant skills can be acquired via education and include a person's innate abilities or talents in a particular area.

What are domain-relevant skills for art directors and writers? You could fill another book with all of them! Art directors, for starters, need to understand the principles of design and layout, appreciate the nuances of typography and know how to use the latest software. Writers must love words, know how to use (and not abuse) a thesaurus and read more than they write. And both of them should bring all the creativity-relevant processes they've got.

Motivation

In life, there are many things we don't enjoy doing. Everyone knows that. What isn't always clear, however, is that we usually don't do things particularly well (or at all!) unless we derive a benefit. Whatever that benefit is, it constitutes our motivation for performing the task.

Creative problem solving requires motivation, too, because it's not easy. It will always take less of your time and energy to apply someone else's solution, to employ the algorithm. That's one of the reasons why you often hear creative thinkers talking about how much they love their work. That passion for whatever they do is a powerful catalyst. It sustains them through periods of difficulty and frustration. It makes success all the more rewarding.

There are two types of motivation. If you are engaged in a task because you find it personally enjoyable and beneficial, that's called *intrinsic motivation*. It comes from within. This form of motivation is clearly linked with your own identity, personality and interests. If you are purely intrinsically motivated, you don't care what anyone else says or thinks. You're doing something because you want to, and that's reason enough.

Sometimes, of course, we do things for other reasons. If you are engaged in a task because you will derive an external benefit, you are (at least to some degree) responding to *extrinsic*

overtaken by something else, perhaps money or fame (extrinsic motivation). Creative performance, like athletic performance, can also suffer the same fate.

Extrinsic motivation isn't inherently bad, as long as intrinsic motivation is primary.

Passion sustains creative thinkers through periods of difficulty and frustration.

motivation. Extrinsic motivations can take many forms, including those that are financial (a paycheck), competitive (a blue ribbon) or social (someone else's approval or favor) in nature. Extrinsic motivation is less connected to who we are as people. Clearly, it has the power to compel us to do things we don't particularly enjoy or want to do. But it isn't always a bad thing. Sometimes, extrinsic forms of motivation can supply us with the extra energy we need to make great achievements.

The fact is that we are typically motivated by both intrinsic and extrinsic forces to think creatively. To ensure the best outcomes, the trick is to know how to keep your motivations properly balanced.

What difference can the right motivation make? Consider a Major League Baseball star that plays for fifteen seasons and makes millions of dollars a year, not counting all of his endorsement deals. He started playing the game when he was five years old and baseball was always his first love. Then one day, unexpectedly, he steps up to the microphone in a crowded press room and announces his retirement. "I'm just not having fun anymore," he tells reporters. Just like that, his career ends. What happened? He loved baseball. But his love of the game (intrinsic motivation) was gradually

Years ago, it was believed that any extrinsic motivation undermined creativity. Today, most scholars agree that extrinsic motivation isn't inherently bad, but it cannot outweigh a person's intrinsic motivation to engage in a creative task. Intrinsic motivation must be primary. But if a product of your own creative thinking (a short story, a new gadget, an ad) wins an award or someone pays you for it, it's okay as long as you don't become preoccupied with those rewards.

That's a liberating idea, given the fact that so many people think creatively as part of their job descriptions. It also reminds us that creative thinking—engaging one's creative process— isn't just a solitary activity. Remember, the usefulness of an idea is part of what makes it creative, and the people around us help make that evaluation. Even though the creative process is richly experienced on a personal level, creativity is also a decidedly social phenomenon.

The Componential Model of Creativity
Teresa Amabile, whom we've already cited in this chapter, is a pioneer in the development of what she calls a "social psychology of creativity." While she acknowledges the value of studying creative thinking on an individual level, she points out the

If a product of your own creative thinking wins an award or someone pays you for it, it's okay as long as you don't become preoccupied with those rewards.

---

lack of research examining social influences on creative performance. Workplace and school environments where creativity is valued, she argues, can make changes that will help people be more creatively productive.

Amabile's work, however, effectively bridges the gap between the scholarship on personal creativity and how it operates in social contexts. Her own Componential Model of Creativity proposes that three factors are necessary for creativity to occur in any domain (a social environment):

1. domain-relevant skills
2. creativity-relevant processes
3. intrinsic motivation for the task

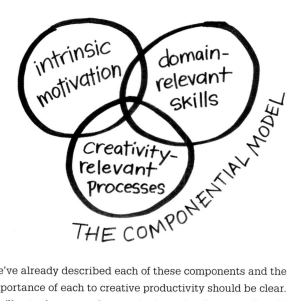

We've already described each of these components and the importance of each to creative productivity should be clear. You'll note, however, that extrinsic motivation is not listed here as a necessary factor. The reason, of course, is because it simply can't be the primary motivation for creative performance. Extrinsic motivators may be everywhere in businesses and schools, but creativity can happen without them. Intrinsic motivation is what's essential.

Students sometimes ask how they can know for sure that advertising is the right career for them. Based on our own experience and what our former students tell us, here's the answer: Advertising is right for you if you believe solving problems with words and images and art and culture

sounds like fascinating work that will make you happy. What's the message? First, happiness matters. Loving what you do makes your whole life better (intrinsic motivation is primary). Second, this business isn't for everyone. Most ad folks work ridiculously long hours and don't make a lot of money or get a lot of glory (extrinsic motivation is secondary). It's tough to be creative every day, on demand, to make someone else rich. If you're doing this kind of work, you'd better be having fun doing it!

UNDERSTANDING ADVERTISING CREATIVITY

As we've noted, creativity is relatively new as a topic in psychological research. Additionally, the teaching and study of advertising as an academic discipline didn't really begin until the 1970s. Given those circumstances, our understanding of advertising creativity is still developing. Because it's difficult to observe the creative process itself, most advertising scholars interested in this area have conducted research dealing with related topics. Take a look at the subjects of some of the most cited research papers in our field relating to creativity:

- defining the creative concept
- risk and creativity
- external evaluations and self-perceptions of creativity
- effects of training on idea-generation
- motivation for creative hobbies
- managerial control of creativity
- creative directors' views on education
- teaching creativity in the undergraduate curriculum

The existing research offers some wonderful insights and represents a broad curiosity about advertising creativity, how it operates, how it is facilitated and how it can be taught. However, we need to do more research that will offer a clearer understanding of the cognitive (read: thinking) dimension. How does the creative process look in the domain of advertising? How do our creative professionals develop ideas? These are important questions that remain largely unanswered.

Setting a New Agenda

For years now, we've been inspired by a 1995 study by Arthur J. Kover, emeritus professor of marketing at Fordham

University. Kover conducted in-depth interviews with fourteen professional advertising writers and asked them to talk about their creative process. This was groundbreaking work. Many of Kover's colleagues didn't believe that the subjects of his study would be able to express their process in words and others questioned whether or not there was an actual process involved with their work in the first place. In spite of these warnings, the study proceeded and it yielded fascinating results. The writers whom Kover interviewed were quite capable of discussing their creative process and did so with great insight and detail. These professionals were thoughtful and reflective about their work. They seemed to possess a keen understanding of their own minds. They held what Kover called "implicit theories" (personal theories about how they did their work), and many of these were similar across interviews. Insights derived from this exploratory study immediately began to reshape our understanding of and appreciation for a creative process adapted to our industry. Kover's work also taught us that, in fact, one can observe and analyze thinking via the collection of first-person, retrospective accounts. He started the methodological ball rolling.

New Models of the Creative Process in Advertising

Emboldened by the knowledge that creative thinking could be studied in this manner, a new study was launched, this time focusing on advertising students learning to become art directors and writers. Glenn Griffin (co-author of this book) wanted to know more about these students' creative process and whether or not their training influenced any change in that process.

In this study, forty-four students at two different universities were each asked to create an ad and to be interviewed two weeks later with their finished ad in hand. During the one-on-one interview sessions, each student was asked to recount the experience of creating the ad. As Kover had already discovered among the professionals who participated in his study, the students were remarkably insightful, articulate and detailed in their descriptions of the process they engaged in to develop the ad. Griffin also observed broad similarities across the students' narratives, which would prove helpful in characterizing the shared elements of their process.

Half of the students interviewed were classified as "beginners" (they had just started their training), and the other half were considered "advanced" (they were preparing to graduate). Because the interviews were conducted with students at different stages in their training, their descriptions of creative process would be compared and any important differences analyzed.

The findings of Griffin's study, published in the *Journal of Advertising*, offered strong evidence that the students' creative process was meaningfully changed as a result of their

training, supporting the idea that creative ability can be nurtured and developed. Two new models of the creative process, as experienced by advertising students, were also proposed: The Performance Model (the creative process at the "beginner" level) and the Mastery Model (the creative process at the "advanced" level).

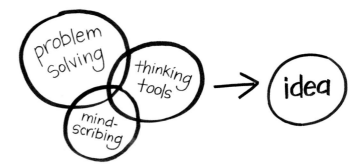

The Performance Model of the creative process.

As beginners, aspiring art directors and writers think of themselves as problem solvers. They like to be given a problem and immediately begin working on solutions. They're learning to use thinking tools as a way to be more mentally productive, but they know and use only a few of them. They make notes and may scribble drawings while thinking—an activity we call "*mindscribing.*" However, they're likely to record only those ideas that they consider potentially viable. "Bad" ideas are typically not written down. The beginners' creative perspective is rooted in advertising. They see themselves as "makers of ads" and their solutions (the ads they create) tend to look and sound like advertising we've all seen before.

In contrast to their less experienced counterparts, advanced students are far less likely to accept a problem as it is presented to them. Instead, they prefer to think about a problem for a while and often decide to redefine the existing problem or find a new one that confronts the client. As they approach the end of their training, advanced students have learned many thinking tools and are more experienced and extensive users of them. They've also come to understand which tools are most useful to them as individuals. They make lots of notes in

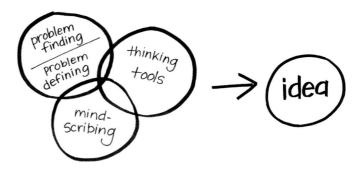

The Mastery Model of the creative process.

their journals while thinking; their mindscribing is unfiltered. Notes and sketches are made without prejudgment of their viability. The advanced students see themselves as "idea people," and they are typically more concerned about the creative quality of an idea than how it will translate into an ad. The idea, instead of the ad, is considered the most important product of thinking. However, once the ad is created, it tends to reflect a more original approach than that of a beginner.

The Performance and Mastery Models, in addition to identifying key dimensions of the advertising creative process as it is developed, raise the following points:

1. It appears that advertising students, over the course of training, are encouraged to become critical thinkers and to make sure that the problem presented to them is the most important one to solve.

2. The acquisition of thinking tools is an important factor in the development of an advertising student's creative process. Individuals test these tools and decide which are the most productive for them.

3. Advertising students learn to stop prejudging their own ideas during the process and keep better notes over time. They come to understand that a viable idea can live anywhere.

4. With experience, advertising students begin to consider the discovery of a great idea (instead of a finished ad) as their ultimate goal. Translation of that idea into an ad is a secondary goal.

Of course, no theoretical model will offer a complete picture of the phenomenon it's intended to describe. However, understanding more about how art directors and writers develop their process is helpful if we intend to study the creative process of their professional counterparts.

WHERE WE'VE BEEN AND WHERE WE'RE GOING

Creativity can be magical, but it isn't magic. It's a method for finding solutions to problems—solutions that reveal our ability to adapt and advance as human beings. And here's the best part: Everyone has the potential to be creative.

People are still learning about the creative process. There's general agreement about how it works in stages and that it operates at both individual and social levels. The process can look different depending on the domain (or line of work) where it happens. Creativity is an act of will that is fueled by passion. It isn't the easiest topic to study. But creative thinkers among us, true to form, are finding ways to tackle it.

The creative process is so crucial to everything we do in advertising (as educators and professionals), but we spend far more time looking at ads than we do thinking about how they were born. We know a little bit about how our students access and develop their creativity because that's where we live. Our next step is to tap the brains of creative pros who do this work and to learn from them. They have so much to share with us.

We're glad you're interested in joining us on this journey. Let's get started.

CHAPTER TWO
PROCESS IS PERSONAL

Just as a workman knows his tools, a musician must know his instrument. A great violinist can perform a solo concerto flawlessly, but she must also possess a keen sense for properly tuning her violin and how it works, from pegbox to chinrest. The investment of so much time and energy breeds an intimate familiarity; a sharpened skill set that separates the player from the virtuoso.

It makes sense that expertise is born of experience. Everything we do presents an opportunity to learn something and perhaps to better understand ourselves as well. This idea is particularly relevant to the day-to-day work of the creative professional. For creative directors, art directors and writers in advertising, the instrument is the mind. If it's your job to make ideas, it's important to understand as much as you can about how your brain works and how to properly tune it for optimal performance. With experience, advertising creatives gradually develop this understanding. They're always learning about how their own minds work. It's a constant revelation.

The funny thing is, most of them don't think about any of this very much. It's all just part of the job, they say.

We find it fascinating. So, we envisioned a different kind of research project several years ago, one that would explore the creative process of professionals in advertising and how they think and feel about that process. As we discussed in chapter one, previous studies, as well as our own research and classroom experiences, told us there was a great story in it. We've

worked with so many talented students over the years and we've interacted with so many amazing creative pros (many of them our former students), and we know how smart and insightful they are.

We started asking questions of any creative director, art director or writer that would listen: What is your creative process? How do you get to an idea?

They had answers for us. Even though the questions might have taken them by surprise or required a bit of deliberation, the considerable self-awareness and intuition we knew would be there revealed itself.

One of the first insights we gained was a crucial one: The creative process is personal. Each person experiences it differently from another, even though we can identify parts of the process that are shared. We also learned that the process, for most, is somewhat predictable or can be expected to follow a familiar protocol. That's not to say, of course, that the pathway to a new idea is ever exactly the same. It's adaptable to the demands of any given situation.

"Generally speaking, I find my process to be a consistent one. It's the specifics that change and evolve. Regardless of the task at hand, I find myself doing the same activities to make it happen. The manner and order in which I do those activities is what changes."

—Shaun Bruce, Art Director,
Amalgamated (New York, New York)

The creative process is personal. Each person experiences it differently from another, even though we can identify parts of the process that are shared.

"The process is like driving a car. It can cruise along, race to a finish, roll up to a scenic overlook and will occasionally require a fill-up. You'll turn the car onto undiscovered roads and end up somewhere that's completely new and exciting. But even though it can go different places, you're still driving a car. The how is the same, but the where is always changing."

—Maggi Machado, Freelance Art Director, Ogilvy & Mather (New York, New York)

"My process is always me thinking really hard about stuff on my own, mixing in a lot of research and talking with relevant people about how to solve the problem, then repeating that process over and over until the finished product is as polished as I can make it."

—David Roth, Copywriter, Crispin Porter + Bogusky (Boulder, Colorado)

"I always immerse myself in the problem, ignore the problem, then address the problem. What does change all the time are the techniques I use when I'm actively engaged in the problem. And really, those techniques tend to change only when I find myself challenged or hitting a wall."

—Ian Simpson, Copywriter, Grip Limited (Toronto, Canada)

"Back when I worked in the Midwest banging out advertising copy on an IBM Selectric, I worked for a guy who accused creative people of something he called 'flight.' 'Flight,' according to him, was something creative people did to avoid working. It included daydreaming, whining, chit-chatting, gossiping, drinking coffee, throwing a Frisbee in the parking lot, leafing through award show annuals, books and magazines, and breathing. Pretty much anything that didn't involve attacking the problem in a completely frontal way. Thirty years later, I'd say 'flight' is how I come up with ideas."

—Joyce King Thomas, Executive Vice President/Chief Creative Officer, McCann Erickson (New York, New York)

It's easy to detect a theme here. Advertising creatives do recognize their own process for developing ideas and can describe it. Furthermore, they generally agree that process can change in response to the problem at hand or as circumstances change. And, importantly, they can articulate how they think. In other words, they know their instrument.

But how does this understanding of one's own cognitive abilities develop in the first place? How can it be used to enhance the creative process? Research in developmental psychology offered some important answers to these questions.

THINKING ABOUT THINKING: THE CONCEPT OF METACOGNITION

John Flavell (b. 1928), emeritus professor of developmental psychology at Stanford University, studied the ways people monitor their own cognitive activities and coined the term "metacognition" to describe how we leverage our own understanding of how we think and how we mentally supervise the achievement of a cognitive (read: thinking) goal.

His work in this area began with a study of preschool and elementary school children investigating their capacity to recognize their own cognitive abilities, such as memory and comprehension. In the study, he asked the children to examine a set of items until they felt confident they had memorized them. The older subjects, after studying the items for a while, said they had memorized the set and then recalled the items perfectly when tested. However, most of the younger students, believing that they were prepared after studying the same set, did not demonstrate perfect recall when tested.

In a 1979 essay describing this research, Flavell noted that preschool-aged children seemed limited in awareness of their own cognitive ability and couldn't accurately evaluate it either. But the elementary school students, as he explained, did demonstrate this awareness and were better able to personally evaluate their cognitive ability. He attributed the difference between age groups to more socialization, more education and more experience with cognitive tasks.

Flavell's work suggests that we gradually become aware of our own cognitive abilities as children and continue to develop this metacognitive knowledge throughout our lives. It also seems intuitive that people who are regularly engaged in thinking tasks and build experience performing those tasks might become more metacognitively aware than those who aren't similarly focused in their day-to-day activities. Could this explain why creative directors, art directors and writers in advertising seem so in touch with how their minds work? Let's explore the theory in more detail.

Metacognition describes how we leverage our own understanding of how we think and how we mentally supervise the achievement of a cognitive goal.

Three Categories of Metacognitive Knowledge

According to Flavell, "metacognitive knowledge consists primarily of knowledge or beliefs about what factors or variables act and interact in what ways to affect the course and outcome of cognitive enterprises." He identifies three categories within this concept: person, task and strategy. They represent the different ways that individuals can guide their own thinking to serve their goals.

The *person* category of metacognitive knowledge covers everything you believe about yourself as a thinker (or about others as thinkers, for that matter). Most of us, over time, can identify preferences for how we learn, what our cognitive strengths and weaknesses are, or how people around us compare in those areas. For example, the knowledge that you can't study for a test in a noisy room would fit in this category. If you believe you're not good at math, or that your best friend is better at math than you are, those are also person variables. This category of knowledge is perhaps the most strongly held of the three and is likely developed over the longest period of time.

> When connecting the person category of metacognitive knowledge to our domain, the professional identities of "art director" and "writer" immediately spring to mind. The career track for advertising creatives is informed by how they look at the world and best express themselves. Writers love words and feel most capable using them to communicate, while art directors embrace the visual and can see all the possibilities there. Some in the industry feel comfortable in both worlds. Many creatives probably began to appreciate these preferences as children and ultimately found a career to complement them.

The *task* category of metacognitive knowledge incorporates your perception of the resources associated with a project. When presented with a task, we make evaluations of the kind of challenge it represents, the quality of available information related to it and what other resources may be required to complete it. For example, if the task presented is unlike any other you've dealt with in the past, you might decide that more time will be required to complete the task in order to accommodate additional study and preparation. If you've previously encountered a similar task and for some reason failed to complete it, you might use that experience to justify using or gathering resources in a different way in hopes of achieving a better outcome. This category of knowledge is applied in response to the unique characteristics of tasks each time they are presented.

> Agency creative pros may juggle a variety of accounts representing many product categories. A writer can be working on ads for radial tires, tax preparation software and a fast-food chain all at the same time. But suppose this writer was hired just last year based on some award-winning work he did for Burger King. Will he draw upon that experience as he makes decisions about what he'll need in order to be successful with a new fast-food client? Probably so. He'll make evaluations about the new task based on his cognitive experiences with the previous task in hopes of developing even stronger ideas.

The *strategy* category of metacognitive knowledge is closely related to the task category, in the sense that it is devoted to the completion of the task. This category incorporates two subcategories of strategy: cognitive and metacognitive. Generally speaking, metacognitive strategies are thought to precede or follow cognitive strategies. They are more about the "big picture" than the moment at hand.

Metacognitive strategies are those we employ to ensure that a goal is achieved or a task is completed. You can think of them as "super strategies" that bolster cognitive strategies.

Notice in the example on the next page that the first (metacognitive) strategy (deciding to study in a quiet room) is employed to make sure the ultimate goal (success on the test) is achieved. The second (cognitive) strategy (reviewing the material) satisfies a more immediate, short-term goal (understanding the material). The third (metacognitive) strategy (asking a friend to quiz you) can be considered a check on the short-term, cognitive strategy and is also employed to make sure the ultimate goal (success on the test) is achieved.

Individuals acquire metacognitive strategies over time and can become more skillful users of them given regular opportunities for application.

METACOGNITIVE STRATEGY	COGNITIVE STRATEGY	METACOGNITIVE STRATEGY
1. You decide to study for your math test in a quiet room because you know noise interferes with your studying.	2. You review all of the material that will be on your math test.	3. You ask a friend to quiz you on the math to assess your understanding prior to the test.

For creative directors, art directors and writers, every new project presents the same fundamental challenge: deliver a great idea that solves the client's problem. This ultimate goal is ever present in a creative's mind, regardless of the details associated with the task. It doesn't really matter what's being sold; the idea is the destination. A typical cognitive strategy might involve making a list of all of a product's benefits to the consumer. Another might be to make a list of all the product's features. However, if the product is very simple (like bubble gum), an art director might decide to dispense with the list making and spend more time developing a personality for the brand. These "executive decisions" that serve as adjustments to the creative process are made all the time. They reflect creative professionals' familiarity with both the task and how their own minds work.

need to build upon previous work. Kover's 1995 study demonstrated advertising writers' ability to characterize their own process, so further investigation of the topic with art directors and creative directors awaited. We knew that these people had the ability to share their experiences; we just needed to listen to them. Second, our own exploratory conversations with creative pros revealed their tendency to manage their own thinking and adapt it to fit a given project. This apparent metacognitive expertise was remarkable and warranted further examination.

One of the main reasons it's difficult to study the creative process is that attempting to observe the process as it happens will inevitably change it somehow. We've seen this again and again. If the goal is to understand creativity in the workplace, we can't reasonably expect to re-create the same phenomenon in a laboratory setting. Furthermore, if people know they're being watched or studied, they tend to perform differently.

One of the main reasons it's difficult to study the creative process is that attempting to observe the process as it happens will inevitably change it somehow.

Metacognition offers a theoretical frame for the proposition that not only do creative professionals in advertising understand their own creative process, but they are sophisticated managers of that process as well. They are people who know their capabilities and can adapt their own ways of thinking to the unique demands of any project. We'd argue that metacognitive awareness is essential to the work that they do. And this theory goes a long way towards explaining why their big ideas seem to be in endless supply.

DESIGNING THE STUDY:
DISCOVERING HOW BIG IDEAS ARE BORN

As we began to design our study of the creative process in advertising, we knew that our work should focus on the individual. This made sense for two reasons. First, there was a

To date, scholars haven't figured out how to observe without being obtrusive.

Which raises the question: If our goal is to understand how a creative director, an art director or a writer develops ideas, should we be preoccupied with trying to observe the process as it happens in the context of solving a particular problem? Given the wide variety of clients and products these professionals encounter, could any isolated case study of their process be realistically characterized as "typical"?

This is why we've come to appreciate the value of retrospective accounts. As evidenced by the rich, detailed descriptions that Kover collected from writers, asking people to talk about their own experiences and then to reflect upon their meaning can yield valuable insights. When individuals are asked to describe the creative process in retrospect, their responses are likely to be informed by the full history of their work, offering a better sense of the phenomenon's most enduring characteristics. Of course, we don't mean to suggest that this method is without its own limitations. There's no way to verify that any personal narrative is completely accurate or comprehensive in describing a thought process. Therefore, to complement first-hand accounts, we decided it would be important to ask each creative professional to provide contact information for a colleague who could describe a study participant's process from an observational perspective. This additional information would enable us to better evaluate the personal narratives.

Because retrospective accounts—coupled with the viewpoints of a creative colleague—would permit us to avoid the significant pitfalls of direct observation techniques, we considered this methodological approach far more viable. The retrospective account constitutes a firsthand description of lived experience and how an individual makes sense of it. Personal perspectives, regardless of their proximity to absolute reality, are certainly valuable in their own right. They lend humanity to the subject matter.

that other forms of communication fail to capture. The "enduring visual product," as described by Scottish researchers Margaret Temple and Chris McVittie, is defined as visual work developed by participants during a research project. These materials, according to Temple and McVittie, offer several important benefits to psychological research:

1. When study participants are encouraged to use visuals as a communication tool, they are given more freedom to respond than a researcher's questions might permit.

2. Visuals may incorporate important dimensions of experience (such as emotions) that aren't as easily or clearly expressed in words.

3. Visuals can provide more subject matter for verbal discussion and analysis.

By asking our study participants to produce a visualization of their own creative process, we could make the project more challenging and potentially enhance the quality of our data. But unlike retrospective accounts, we didn't have any existing evidence that asking people to draw their process would be as useful. Ultimately, we decided that the sheer novelty of the

---

When individuals are asked to describe the creative process in retrospect, their responses are likely to be informed by the full history of their work, offering a better sense of the phenomenon's most enduring characteristics.

Having decided that the collection of personal narratives about the creative process would constitute a primary methodology for our project, we then considered a couple of other issues. The success of our study would hinge upon the consent and participation of a very smart, talented (and insanely busy) group of professionals. We're realists: We understand that the prospect of participation in academic research isn't all that exciting. So, we needed a way to make this project more challenging and—dare we say it—fun. In true advertising fashion, we thought about our audience: people who sell things with artful combinations of words and visuals. There's an idea, we thought. What if we asked participants in our study to do more than just talk about their creative process? What if they were asked to illustrate it, too?

As it turns out, we weren't the first researchers to consider the potential value of this technique as a supplement to other methods. From the scholarship in art therapy, we learned that visual images are often used to explore human experiences

request was reason enough to make it part of our study. We had no idea what was in store.

When we tested this method with a few of our friends in the industry, the reaction was one of both surprise and fascination. The visual challenge, originally considered as a supplement to interviews, captured the imagination in ways we hadn't anticipated. We realized that the excitement generated by asking professionals to illustrate their process could greatly enhance participation in the study. So, we decided to run with it.

The Creative Process Illustrated—also known as "you know, that drawing-your-process-project we've been talking about" in the hallways of many ad agencies—was born.

Choosing the Study Participants

Admittedly, and from the very beginning, we were interested in studying a special "brand" of advertising creativity: the kind that yields very good work. There are a number of ways

There's an idea, we thought. What if we asked participants in our study to do more than just talk about their creative process? What if they were asked to illustrate it, too?

to define what's "very good" out there. We started by scouring the credit listings of work that appeared in leading industry award books (*Communication Arts Advertising Annual*, the *Art Directors Club Annual*, *The One Show Annual*, *Lürzer's Archive*). We thought about campaigns that were brave, innovative, socially responsible or otherwise notable for the right reasons, and scribbled down more names. We made a wish list of advertising's living legends and hoped that a few of them might play along. And, of course, as teachers, we thought about the next generation of creatives—the art directors and writers still in the early stages of their careers but already making their mark.

The final list we compiled, approaching three hundred names, was compelling because it represented so many good people and so much brainpower. (Unfortunately, the list suffered in gender balance and racial/ethnic diversity—the industry must do better in those areas.) Our "sample" was certainly not randomly selected. Instead, we sought out the best and hoped for a good response, fingers crossed.

Creating the Problem
We developed, designed and mailed a study packet to all the creative pros on our list. Each packet contained a letter explaining the project, a poster-sized (17" x 22" [43cm x 56cm]) "Process Canvas" with a twin-tipped, black Sharpie marker to facilitate the participant's drawing of the creative process and a postage-paid return envelope. The back of the "Process Canvas" included a series of questions, a consent form and the following instructions:

1. Think about your own creative process. Think about the route you take to find ideas.

2. Experiment with illustrating that process on a scratch piece of paper. Can your visualization (with or without words) offer someone else an understanding of the process as you experience it?

3. When you are satisfied with your solution, use the Sharpie marker (provided) to transfer it to the Process Canvas on the reverse of this sheet.

4. Fold this sheet and mail it back to us in the postage-paid return envelope we've provided to you. Thanks for your participation!

About seventy-five drawings were returned to us over the course of a year. From that collection, a subset was chosen to appear in this book.

Reactions to the Project
Most of the recipients of our study packet expressed some surprise at what we asked them to do. Even though they use their creative process on a daily basis, many admitted that they had never really considered it objectively or imagined how it might look on paper. But the challenge to do so was intriguing to them. We heard from some folks who started, re-started and never finished. Many of those who completed and returned their drawings described the task as difficult but enjoyable at the same time. It helped them learn some things about themselves. The level of self-analysis and introspection represented in the drawings is remarkable. Plus, several contributors were curious to see what others' processes looked like and how they compared.

"It's pretty tough to visualize the process, but it's fun to actually think about."

—Adrian Alexander, Writer,
Third Culture Kidz, (Austin, Texas)

"It was fun and harder than I thought."

—Ian Cohen, Co-Founder/Creative
Director, Wexley School for Girls,
(Seattle, Washington)

"This sat on my desk for several days, giving me vague anxiety—just like any creative assignment I really want to do well. And waiting is good: First ideas can be awfully literal and ugly. So what does thinking up good ideas look like? It's a really good question and I'm not sure I've exactly answered it."

—Andy Hall, Freelance Writer/
Creative Director (New York, New York)

"Who says research can't be fun?"

—Mike Heid, Writer, Peter A. Mayer
Advertising (New Orleans, Louisiana)

"I am very excited to get a peek at how great thinkers do their jobs."

—David T. Jones, Chief Creative Officer,
Third Street; Cartoonist, *Adweek*
(Chicago, Illinois)

"This process has been both intimidating and inspiring—my favorite combination."

—Nancy Rice, Founding Partner, Fallon McElligott Rice (Minneapolis, Minnesota)

As is true with most research, we didn't achieve 100 percent participation. We did a great deal of e-mail reminding, phone begging and the like in order to increase our numbers. There are still many creative stars out there whose drawings we'd love to see. If you're one of them and reading this, can't you see how cool this is? Call us and let's talk.

What a Collection!

Upon reviewing the process drawings and the personal and colleague narratives, we began to appreciate this "data" as a highly unique and enlightening archive. The responses we received surprised us in their variety, clarity and candor. While the drawings confirm the notion that no two individuals' minds work exactly the same way, we do find significant overlap in the nature of experiences. Art directors, writers and creative directors all share many of the same fears, agree about the most frustrating aspects of their jobs and even use some of the same strategies for doing good work.

Every contributor to our study helped us better understand the creative process in advertising as both an intensely personal and a surprisingly universal phenomenon. Big ideas, it seems, are the products of wonderfully diverse personalities and their one-of-a-kind brains. But across the spectrum, we can recognize shared truths, frustrations, priorities and other characteristics that are part of every process.

You really have to see it to believe it, as they say. Are you ready?

CHAPTER THREE

PROCESS ILLUSTRATED: THE COLLECTION

To try and understand the creative process in advertising is to try and capture the ephemeral. Every writer's, every art director's, every creative director's process is intensely personal and (as we learned) quite challenging to explain to someone else, particularly when it isn't anything one ever expected to try to do. People who make advertising are prepared to bring their ideas to the table and to have others love, hate, poke at, change, buy, steal or reject them. They've learned to handle criticism, to constantly revise and remake, and to win or lose a client's business. But when asked to share their understanding of how they think and where their ideas come from, even the most seasoned pros seem surprised, maybe even a little intimidated, by the question.

Exceptionally talented creative people in this industry can be found everywhere. Some are working in advertising agencies, others are running their own shops, and a growing number are freelancing. Some work with multimillion-dollar clients and others cater to small businesses. Regardless of their salaries, their agency's annual billings or whether or not they've ever created a Super Bowl spot, the people doing the best work in advertising have a way of getting noticed. They win local, then regional, then national ADDY Awards. Their work shows up in *Communication Arts* or *Lürzer's Archive*. A New York agency steals them from a shop in Minneapolis (or the other way around). Next year, they'll be on a Clio shortlist. These are the people who build myth and shape culture with their work. They are the reason your mom loves that commercial or your

little sister can't stop singing it. They are the people who've decided that advertising is a profession nobler than its reputation suggests, and they work hard every day to prove it.

They are great thinkers. We should all know more about them.

We believed that by saying, "show me" to these idea makers, people for whom bravery and the love of a challenge are critical to their expertise, we could get some amazing answers. And we did.

This unique collection, this archive of advertising's creative brain trust, runs the gamut with respect to age, background, agency history, clients, awards and life experience. A few of the people you'll read about are living legends. Some are on that trajectory. Others are just getting started in their careers but are already turning heads.

Learn about their backgrounds by reading their professional bios. See samples of their work (there's a lot that you will recognize). Let the people with whom they've worked—their partners—tell you what it's like. Most importantly, take this opportunity to see some of advertising's brightest creative minds laid out on each process canvas presented here. (We offer a few of our own insights about those, too.)

Whether you're a student of the craft, at work in the agency world, or just a great fan of advertising and curious about how creative people in this business do their jobs, you will be inspired.

CHRIS ADAMS

GROUP CREATIVE DIRECTOR, TBWA\CHIAT\DAY (LOS ANGELES, CALIFORNIA)

TBWA\CHIAT\DAY

If you've gotten choked up watching a dog food ad in the last couple of years, it's probably thanks to Chris Adams. His words and creative vision transformed Pedigree into the dog food company that loves dogs, building a cult following (just survey dog lovers' blogs) and a place in advertising history.

Looking back, maybe he failed accounting at the University of Maryland for a reason. Maybe those vintage white pearl

Ludwig drums he got for Christmas in the fourth grade were his inspiration to do something different. Whatever it was that drove him to find classes where he could get in his own head and explore, Adams thought it would be fun to give the advertising program a try. In 1994, he started an internship at Chiat/Day (mostly because he needed it to graduate).

In fact, Adams claims a distinction that few creative directors can: He's risen through the ranks at the same agency since he graduated, working in the Jacksonville, Florida, and Washington, DC, Chiat offices before making his way to Los Angeles in 2000. He's created work for Nissan and Infiniti, helped Steve Jobs introduce iMacs and iPods and, most recently, charmed the world with the "Dogs Rule" campaign for Pedigree.

Over the years, his work has remained compelling and authentic, never formulaic. "I find myself breaking the rules

» "TAP PROJECT"
SAFE DRINKING WATER WEBSITE

Agency: TBWA\Chiat\Day, Los Angeles Chief
Creative Officer Worldwide: Lee Clow Chief
Creative Officer: Rob Schwartz Group Creative
Directors: Chris Adams, Margaret Keene
Associate Creative Director: Scott McFarlin
Art Director: Paulo Cruz Writer: Ted Kapusta
Client: UNICEF United States Fund

a lot," Adams explains. "I think a lot of creative people do."
He's been recognized by the Cannes Lions International
Advertising Festival, *Communication Arts*, D&AD and The
One Show. And he's won best of show at the OBIE Awards
and the $100,000 Grand Prize MPA Kelly Award (the money
was donated to the Pedigree Dog Adoption Drive). In 2008,
he judged The One Show.

When he's not at the office, you can find him on a wave, on the
soccer pitch, on his third glass of red wine with his beautiful
wife, or on the couch napping with his dog and two cats.

Process
"For me, the process begins with just filling my head with stuff.
Devouring media, soaking up the world around me—words
and images and music and life. Not because I have a particular assignment that I need them for, but just because I enjoy it.
Then, when I sit down to think about ideas for a client, I've got
all this stuff bubbling around in my head. There's all this stimuli in there for my thoughts to bounce around on. Sometimes
the big idea literally just jumps right out. Other times I have
to be more patient, little ideas have to eat up other little ideas
and merge with other notions until they're big and strong and
can make it on their own. Often, I can't find the ideas myself,
and my partner is the one who discovers the ideas locked up in
my own head."

—Chris Adams

Partner
"Chris keeps a regular-sized black journal, and during a
meeting when we're getting briefed on an assignment, he'll

sometimes scribble little illegible parts and pieces there. This
little thought incubates in his mind for a while. Sometimes, I'll
find it and sprinkle a little fairy dust on it. Then he'll open his
computer, pull up a Word file, and, as he puts it, 'it pretty much
writes itself.' That's it. Not sure if the end result has anything
to do with the original scribble, but what it turns out to be is
a fully-formed, strategically sound, beautifully articulated reason to believe in whatever it is we're trying to sell.

"Many creatives are petulant egomaniacs, willing to forego
real insights and truths in order to further their own creative
agendas. Chris couldn't do that if he tried. If the project is worthy (and even when it's not), he's compelled to find something
special about it and turn it into an engaging piece of communication. He's the best kind of partner, always giving ideas freely
and embracing them eagerly, then tweaking them perfectly."

—Margaret Keene, Group Creative Director,
TBWA\Chiat\Day

INSIGHTS FROM THE PROCESS CANVAS

You've got to stock the pond to keep the fishing good. Feed
your head and it will work harder for you.

A fly fisherman is an artist with tools, carefully landing the
best of the lot. The metaphor implies the importance of
craftsmanship and precision.

Funneling is a necessary practice. Great volumes of information must be distilled or condensed as solutions get closer.

Meet Echo.

Echo lives in a shelter.
She was the loser in a divorce.
Echo isn't used to her new home,
the cement feels strange on her paws.
When people walk past she runs
to the front of her cage and smiles.
Then they move on.
And Echo slumps back down.
When you buy PEDIGREE,
we make a donation to help dogs
like Echo find loving homes.
Help us help dogs.
The PEDIGREE Adoption Drive

Pedigree | Dogsrule.com

⌃ "DOGS RULE" BILLBOARD

Agency: TBWA\Chiat\Day, Los Angeles
Chief Creative Officer Worldwide: Lee Clow
Creative Directors: Duncan Milner, Eric
Grunbaum **Associate Creative Director/
Art Director:** Margaret Keene **Writer:** Chris
Adams **Client:** Mars Petcare US, Inc.

« "ADOPTION DRIVE" MAGAZINE AD

Agency: TBWA\Chiat\Day, Los Angeles
Chief Creative Officer Worldwide: Lee Clow
Creative Directors: Margaret Keene, Chris
Adams **Art Directors:** Jera Mehrdad, Jeremy
Boland **Writers:** Marcin Markiewicz, Eric
Terchila **Client:** Mars Petcare US, Inc.

PEDIGREE® and DOGS RULE® are registered trade-
marks of Mars, Incorporated and its affiliates. The
copyright in the PEDIGREE® advertisements displayed
herein is owned by Mars, Incorporated. These trade-
marks and the PEDIGREE® advertisements are used
with permission. Mars, Incorporated is not associated
with the publisher.

ADRIAN ALEXANDER

WRITER, THIRD CULTURE KIDZ (AUSTIN, TEXAS)

Writer Adrian Alexander and art director Rochelle Raiss consider the business of freelance.

Third Culture Kidz

Adrian Alexander lives in a good place. It's that cross-road where opportunity meets talent, a place where work is play and play just happens to build your career. After all, he's a writer.

"I could've taken such a different path," he says. His German mother gave him a penchant for cooking and languages. His African-American father instilled a love of art and writing. Still, he thought he'd be a scientist when he was growing up. Then, in college, he found advertising. At his senior year portfolio critique, Alexander was offered a job at a small boutique agency in Houston. He accepted, but he soon found that Houston wasn't for him. What should a writer do?

He moved to Europe. By the time he returned a year later after traveling the continent, he had a job offer from Crispin Porter + Bogusky in Miami. A few months later, he moved again, this

Step 1

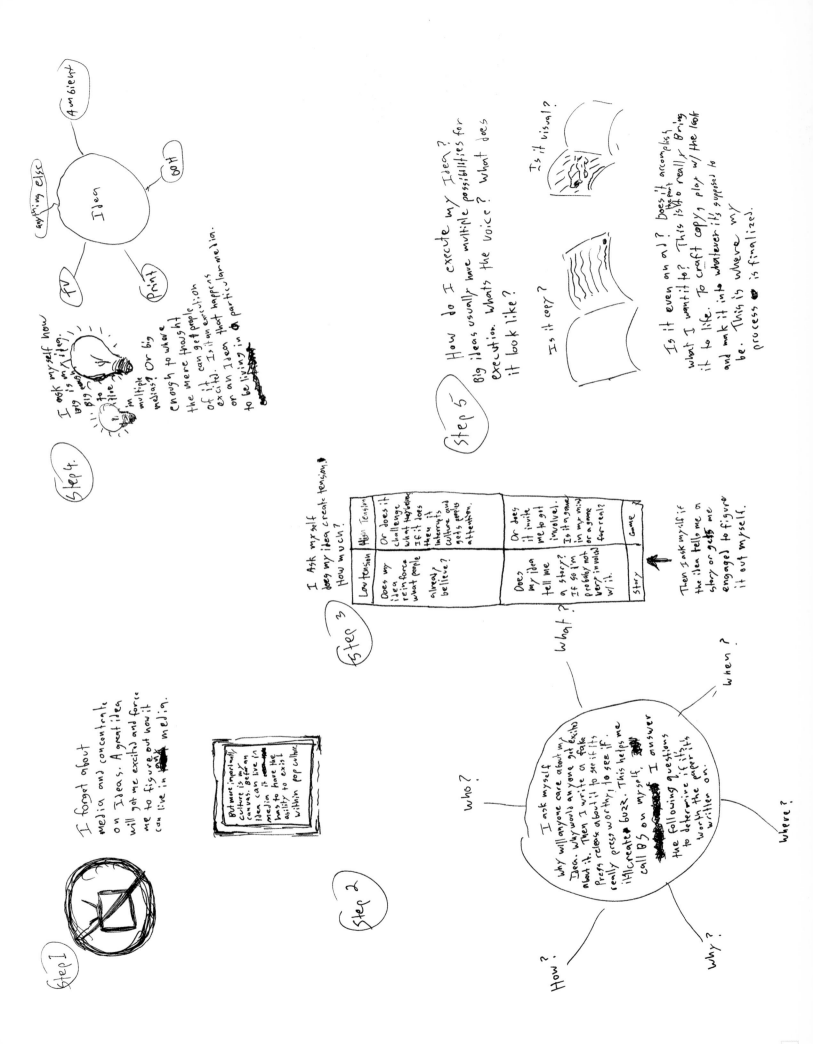

I forget about media and concentrate on Ideas. A great idea will got me excited and force me to figure out how it can live in [any] media.

> But most importantly culture is my canvas. Before an idea can live in media it [must] have the ability to exist within pop culture.

Step 2

I ask myself Why will anyone care about my Idea. Why would anyone get excited about it. Then I write a fake press release about it to see if it really press worthy. This helps me [increate] buzz. I call BS on myself. I answer the following questions to determine if it's worth the paper it's written on.

Who? · How? · Why? · Where? · When? · What?

Step 3

I Ask myself does my idea create tension? How much?

	Low Tension	High Tension
Story	Does my idea reinforce what people already believe?	Or does it challenge what they believe? If it does then it interrupts culture and gets people attention.
Game	Does my idea tell me a story? If so I'm probably not very involved with it.	Or does it invite me to get involved. Is it a game in my mind or a some for-real?

Then I ask myself if the idea tells me a story or gets me engaged to figure it out myself.

Step 4

I ask myself how Big is my idea. Big enough to [live] in multiple medias? Or big enough to where the mere thought of it can get people excited on an execution. Is it an execution of it). Is it an idea that happens on multiple media. or an idea that happens in [a] particular media to be living in particular media.

Idea — Ambient · anything else · 60H · Print · TV

Step 5

How do I execute my idea? Big ideas usually have multiple possibilities for execution. Whats the voice? What does it look like?

Is it copy? · Is it visual?

Is it even on ad? Does it accomplish the point, what I want it to? This is to really bring it to life. To craft copy/s plot w/ the look and make it into whatever it's supposed to be. This is where my process is finalized.

> **Those in the business of making ads will always be limited by the size of their budgets, but those in the business of creating ideas will be limited only by the scope of their imaginations.**

time to Boulder, Colorado, where the agency opened a new office. Alexander admits that his time at Crispin was the most influential period of his young career, and led him to view problem solving in media-neutral ways and to make messages that are surprisingly compelling.

Two years later—with work for Coca-Cola Zero and Giro helmets under his belt—Alexander and his art director partner, Rochelle Raiss, moved to Austin. The name of their shop, Third Culture Kidz, is an homage to the post-postmodern freelance lifestyle.

Process

"At some point I asked myself, 'Am I in the business of making ads, or am I in the business of creating ideas?' And yes, there is a difference. Making ads forces one to think inside conventional media boxes. Ideas, on the other hand, aren't bound by the rules of advertising. They can transcend the conventional constraints, and if they're big enough, even infiltrate hearts, minds and culture as a whole. Those in the business of making ads will always be limited by the size of their budgets, but those in the business of creating ideas will be limited only by the scope of their imaginations. Because great ideas don't need mass communication to be heard; their mere existence is enough to get people talking. As a result, they diffuse through culture organically. In other words, when you're in the business of creating great ideas, people become your 'media.' So, with this in mind, maybe you should ask yourself, 'Which business are you in?' I, for one, am going with the latter."

—Adrian Alexander

Partner

"Every now and then life throws us one of those rare coincidences. Mine happened when Adrian and I started our new job on the same day. We quickly realized that we both had a similar upbringing—we share a German heritage, and we both speak the language. Also, we both worked at CP+B, and we share a common desire to not settle for mediocrity. As a result, we're constantly challenging one another. But more than anything else, no matter what this business throws at us, we always find a way to make each other laugh. It's how every great partnership should work."

—Rochelle Raiss, Art Director,
Third Culture Kidz

INSIGHTS FROM THE PROCESS CANVAS

Organizing and visualizing data is important in determining a path; that is, working out your strategy in pictures and words.

Many questions lead to many answers and, sometimes, to even more questions.

Advertising is never created in a vacuum. The phrase "culture is my canvas" emphasizes the importance of context.

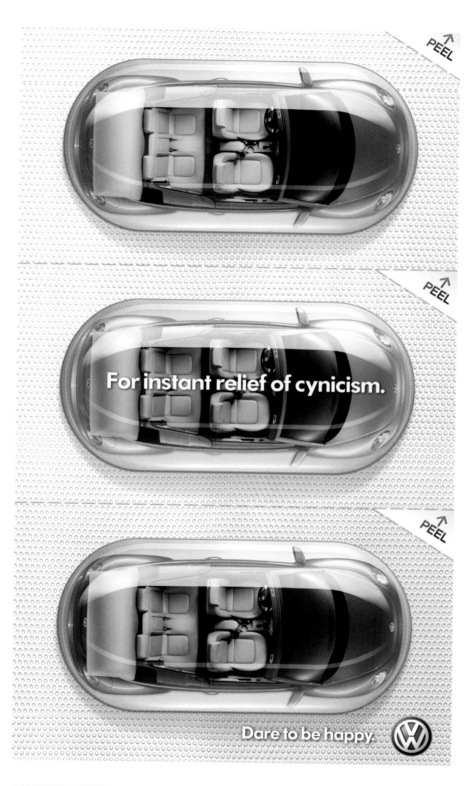

⌃ "DARE TO BE HAPPY"
MULTIMEDIA CONCEPT

Agency: Crispin Porter + Bogusky **Art Director:**
Laura Hausman **Writer:** Adrian Alexander
Client: Volkswagen®

The Volkswagen® trademark is used with permission
of Volkswagen Group of America, Inc.

ANDY AZULA

SENIOR VICE PRESIDENT/CREATIVE DIRECTOR, THE MARTIN AGENCY (RICHMOND, VIRGINIA)

THE MARTIN AGENCY

Yes, you've seen that guy somewhere before. Andy Azula is the creative-director-turned-UPS-spokes-character who's become famous starring in his own work. Oddly enough, he never auditioned for the gig. After several casting calls, UPS executives and focus groups decided they liked Azula's delivery (pardon the pun) better than any of the actors', and a star was born.

Even though Azula gets recognized on the street more often these days, his name was already well known in the advertising business. Prior to becoming the senior vice president and creative director of The Martin Agency, Azula worked at Goodby, Silverstein & Partners and McCann Erickson in San Francisco; Fallon Worldwide in Minneapolis; and Loeffler Ketchum Mountjoy (LKM) in Charlotte, North Carolina. He has been involved in developing campaigns for Microsoft, BMW, Lee Jeans, Nikon, Budweiser and the *Wall Street Journal*, to name a few. His work has been recognized by *Communication Arts*, The One Show, Cannes Lions International Advertising Festival, the National ADDY Awards, the Clios, the MPA Kelly Awards, and the magazines *Archive*, *Graphis* and *Print*. He also sits on the board of The One Club for Art & Copy.

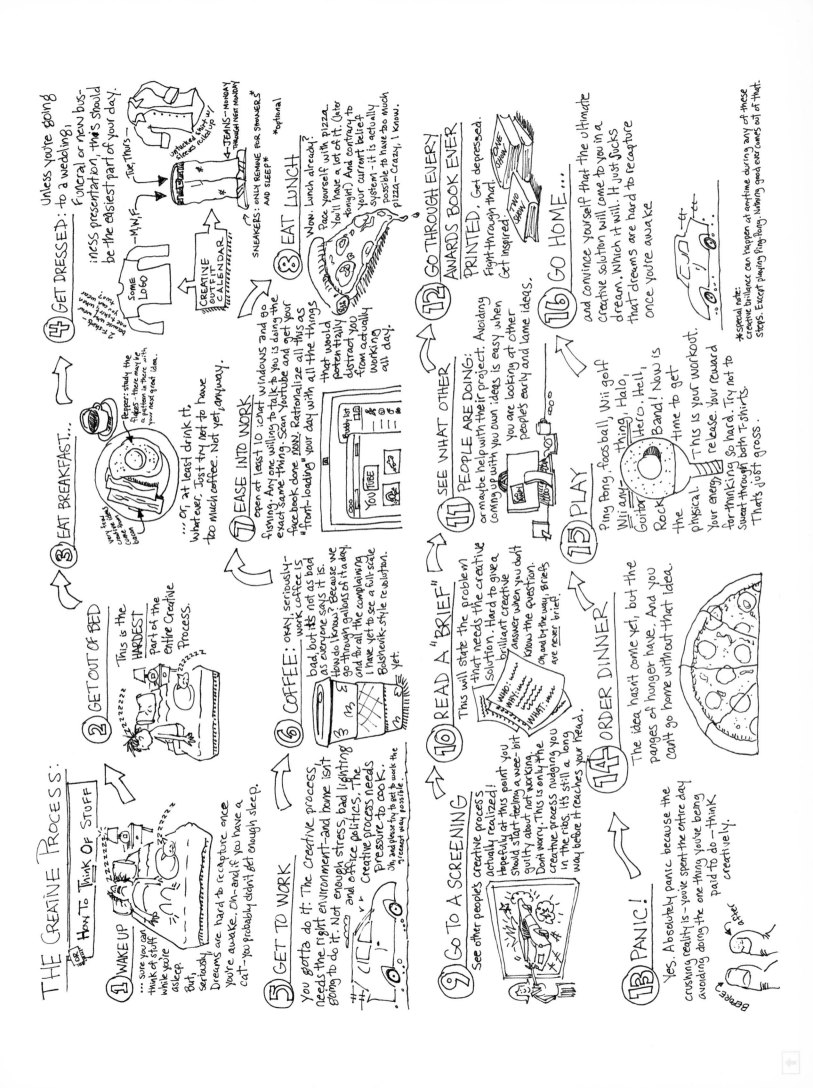

Spend some time, no matter how counterintuitive it seems to your gut and to the deadline, and figure out what the problem really is.

Process

"Remember the dreaded blank piece of paper? It's become the blank Word doc, the blank InDesign page and the blank Photoshop canvas.

"But the beauty of these things is that they are just that: blank slates. Chances for originality. Chances to create movements. Opportunities to make a difference. Opportunities to fail.

"For me, the process of creativity is messy, chaotic and disorganized. There is only a certain amount of science to it. So, I think it's important to start there. Use that little bit of 'science' to build the wings before you jump off the cliff of thinking. And the easiest way to do that is to resist the urge to jump in the first place. That's right. Spend some time, no matter how counterintuitive it seems to your gut and to the deadline, and figure out what the problem really is. Because the better you understand the actual problem, the easier it is to deliver a solid, memorable and creative answer. Or, to even deliver a whole new opportunity. Shocking, I know. But you'd be surprised how many wrong answers are out there. The right answers are those that we remember, make us laugh, make us love, and that move us.

"And remember that dreaded blank page? Well, look... it's filled. Now that wasn't so bad, was it?"

—Andy Azula

Partner

"Andy came to The Martin Agency with a very impressive résumé in tow, so the expectations were pretty high when we first started working together on UPS ... and he did not disappoint. And I'm not just referring to the work itself, because that goes without saying. What impressed me the most was how he immersed himself into UPS's business; to really understand their business problems at the core and how their diverse products and services needed to be communicated in order to solve those problems. That's a daunting task considering UPS's global size and scope, but Andy took on that personal challenge and emerged with a better understanding of what UPS does than all of the people who had worked on the business for the past three years. He then takes that knowledge and blends it with his unique creativity, which results in business-improving work for the client.

"I've had the pleasure of actually working alongside him during the creation of some of our whiteboard spots, and I'm truly amazed each time. It's fascinating to watch his mind work. Whether it's his own idea or improving someone else's, Andy continually reverts back to the business and campaign objectives to make the work better. The clients can see and appreciate the thought that goes into each Azula-inspired TV spot or print ad, which builds the trust and confidence that Andy is a steward of their brand and is genuinely looking out for their best interests. It's not about creative awards; it's about the results. And that's what makes Andy such a rare talent in today's world of self-promotion and 'me-first' attitudes.

"I'm proud to call him my colleague and friend."

—Tedd Aurelius, Vice President and
Account Director, The Martin Agency

INSIGHTS FROM THE PROCESS CANVAS

Life and work inevitably intersect, particularly when you work sixty-hour weeks, give or take twenty hours. It can become difficult to separate the two.

Guess what? Senior-level creatives still panic. Years of experience build confidence and craft, but even seasoned pros feel the pressure to find that next great idea.

So you want to make advertising? Here's hoping you like pizza and coffee—the breakfast, lunch and dinner of creative champions.

⌃ "BUDDY LEE" MAGAZINE AD

Headline: Another reason we're able to say, "NO DOLLS WERE INJURED IN THE MAKING OF OUR COMMERCIALS." **Agency:** Fallon Worldwide, Minneapolis **Creative Director:** Harvey Marco **Art Director:** Andy Azula **Writer:** Greg Hahn **Client:** Lee Jeans

© 1990 Lee Jeans, a division of VF Jeanswear Limited Partnership

DAVID BALDWIN

LEAD GUITAR, BALDWIN& (DURHAM, NORTH CAROLINA)

baldwin&

How does it feel to be at the top of your game? David Baldwin, one of the most awarded writers and creative directors in the advertising and branding business today, recently formed Baldwin&, a project-oriented creative shop in Durham, North Carolina. Baldwin is there, at the top, inventing and wondering how to do the next big thing. That's how he works. His entrepreneurial agency model is a natural result of his noteworthy work around the country, where over the last couple of decades he crafted smart advertising at Deutsch in New York, Hal Riney in San Francisco, Cole & Weber United in Portland, Oregon, and Leonard/Monahan in Providence, Rhode Island.

At McKinney (also in Durham), his creative leadership resulted in global visibility for the agency and a stretch of award show honors that make other agencies envious. Baldwin also served as the chairman of The One Club for Art & Copy, the force

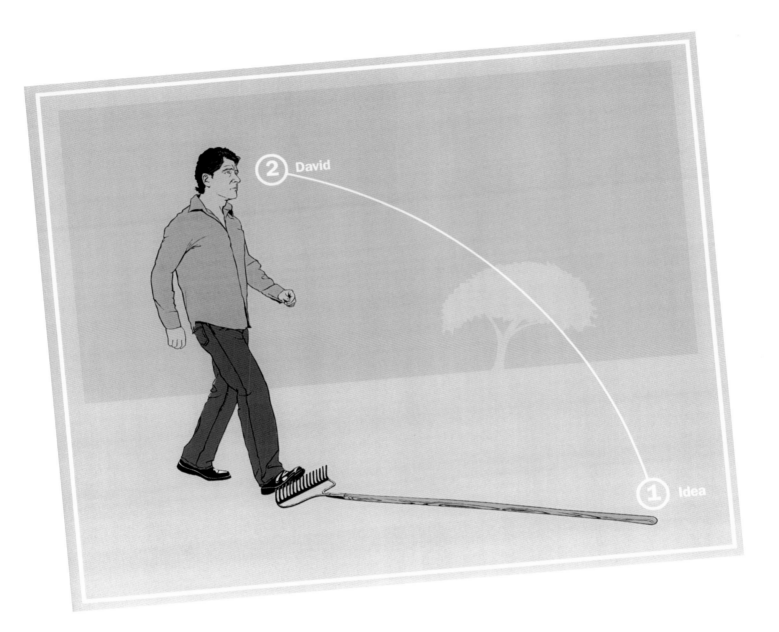

I just spew and spew thoughts, write them down, and then the trick is figuring out which ones are any good.

behind The One Show, for five years. In that role, he was a champion for the best in advertising and the profession, urging creatives to new levels of innovation, responsibility and leadership in the advertising world. That's how fame pays it forward.

Baldwin's creative life extends beyond advertising. He's an executive producer on the film *Art & Copy*, which premiered at the 2009 Sundance Film Festival. And, there's always his music gig to fall back on. He's a guitarist and songwriter for the band Pants, whose album, *Twice the Snake You Need*, was released recently.

Process

"I'd love to say that it's hard work and discipline that lead to great ideas, but it's a much wispier process than that. Ideas just kind of happen for me. I look at it like this: Great ideas are already out there, you just have to find them. So I just spew and spew thoughts, write them down, and then the trick is figuring out which ones are any good. I have noticed that I think differently when I'm talking versus sitting, writing by myself. I'm able to make more interesting leaps and connections. I call it working by conversation. It's always worked for me."

—David Baldwin

Partner

"When David approves your idea, it really means you're only at the beginning of the process.

"This is because he loves to poke things. At no point in the process is he done poking, and, therefore, neither are you. Poke, poke. And when you're both done poking things, it's only because it's time for the piece to run. Often, the only

similarity between the original idea and the final product is the client's name. (If it's something you filmed, then some of the locations might vaguely make the cut.)

"And you know what? It's usually better than what you presented.

"An example (a non-advertising one): The idea was to get together and play instruments after work. Pretty solid.

"Poke. Poke, poke.

"Cut to a year later. I'm crouched onstage at the Rock and Roll Hall of Fame, wearing tight leather pants and mascara, shrieking in David Lee Rothian falsetto in front of a packed house as David plays a blistering guitar solo with one hand and eats a sandwich with the other as a TV camera swoops by on a crane.

"See? Better."

—Mitch Bennett, Associate Creative
Director and Writer, GSD&M, Austin,
Texas; Guitarist, Pants

INSIGHTS FROM THE PROCESS CANVAS

Breaking the rules is sometimes part of the process. Ask a pro for a doodle, get a polished illustration in return.

Some of the most talented creatives in the business make it look easy. But don't be fooled.

The best ideas are sometimes the ones you never saw coming.

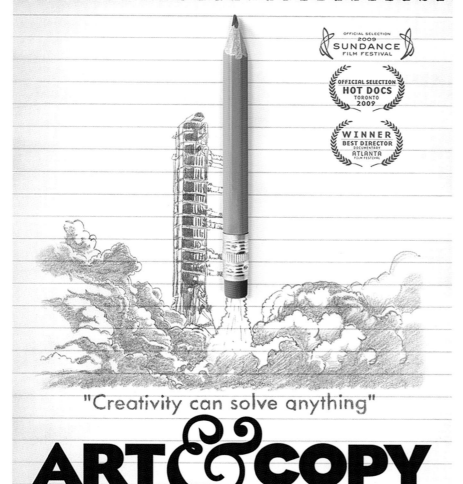

« "ART & COPY" DOCUMENTARY

Executive Producers: David Baldwin, Gregory Beauchamp, Kirk Souder, Mary Warlick (based on an original concept by Gregory Beauchamp and Kirk Souder) **Director:** Doug Pray **Cinematographer:** Peter Nelson **Editor:** Philip Owens **Original Score:** Jeff Martin **Producers:** Jimmy Greenway, Michael Nadeau

An Art & Industry and Granite Pass Production. © 2009 The One Club.

Poster Design: Mike Hughes of Butler, Shine, Stern & Partners (Sausalito, California)

DUSTIN BALLARD

WRITER, THE RICHARDS GROUP (DALLAS, TEXAS)

In 2004, *Adweek* called Dustin Ballard one of the "best creatives you've never heard of." Since then, Ballard has been working hard to buck that title. Since he graduated from the University of Texas at Austin in 2003, his writing has been recognized by The One Show, the Cannes Lions International Advertising Festival, the ANDY Awards, the London International Awards and *Communication Arts*. In 2007, Ballard was one of twelve art directors and writers under thirty years old selected by the Clio Future Gold | Young Creatives Program to elevate and inspire young talent in the industry. That's what you call a running start.

Ballard began his career at Crispin Porter + Bogusky, where he worked on Mini Cooper, Virgin Atlantic, Burger King and the American Legacy Foundation's "Truth" anti-smoking campaign. He sold his first television script to a client to which he wasn't assigned. Sixteen spots and two years later, that

KEY

· Small idea
• OK idea
● Pretty good idea
⬤ Big idea

initiative paid off. In 2006, the Texas native joined The Richards Group in Dallas, where he works on the Chick-fil-A, Orkin and Amstel Light accounts, as well as new business pitches.

An accomplished fiddle player, Ballard also won first place at the Battle of the Ad Bands in New York. In this business, it's smart to have a second career already mapped out.

Process

"My brain hates creativity. Like most cerebrums, mine spends 99 percent of its day following pre-worn thought paths and shortcuts. I don't re-invent the way I brush my teeth every morning. My brain would disown me.

"For me, advertising is a battle against my brain. A battle against process itself. It's not about accumulating a toolbox of 'tricks' to reach a solution; it's about finding the truth behind what you're saying and throwing everything else out. With that said, there are a few rules I do like to follow:

"Drift off course. For me, getting off topic is a defense mechanism. La La Land is where my mind resets itself so I can pounce on an idea with fresh eyes. It's not about losing focus; it's about avoiding the frustration and close-mindedness that comes from chaining yourself to a brief for three hours.

"Don't settle. The way I figure, if an idea doesn't excite me, it won't excite a stranger whose TV show I just interrupted. Don't stop at the first workable idea you have. It's not the best.

"Learn to 'love 'em and leave 'em.' Many of my favorite ideas have died for awfully silly reasons. It's just a universal fact of advertising. Some creatives spend their time sulking. Others strike back with even better ideas.

"Finally, don't live in a bubble. Those who are cultural sponges are the most interesting people. And interesting people have interesting ideas. Explore. Learn. Listen. Let the world improve your advertising; don't make advertising your world."

—Dustin Ballard

Partner

"Dustin is the best writer I know. His creative process is something I can count on even though it differs with each new challenge. I can count on him to stay calm. His ability to avoid becoming distracted by his emotions (being frazzled, whiny or moody… unlike many other brilliant creatives) keeps his focus on the real question at hand: How do we make this great?

"Dustin is a brilliant fiddle player. I believe he also uses that part of his brain to fuel his creative process. When writing, he keeps in mind that the best songs (and ads) are ones that surprise. They must grab you and make you remember something, make you feel something.

"He doesn't stop until all of the pieces fit. Until they sing.

"When we work together, there is a rhythm. He doesn't stop with one thought. He leads it to the next, and the next. Never a naysayer, he suggests, 'Let's try it,' or 'Let's build on it.' At bumps in the road, we take time to walk away from the idea, and go run around outside, act goofy and let our inner kid take over. Sometimes, that's the secret to finding the best stuff: Leave it be.

"Dustin knows that developing great work is the (relatively) easy (well, sorta) part of the job. Selling it is the hard part. One of the things I appreciate about Dustin is his flair for presentation. Sometimes, creative teams feel the need to offer clients an over-the-top song and dance when trying to sell them on an idea. Dustin wants the work to sell itself—with a little nudge, if necessary.

"I call Dustin 'The Silent Killer.' He's the soul of calm, modesty and focus while doing great work that everyone wants to emulate."

—Jill Efrussy, Art Director,
The Richards Group

INSIGHTS FROM THE PROCESS CANVAS

Ideas come in different sizes. Those big ideas are good ones because they hold the greatest potential to solve big problems.

Notice the "key." Writers want to be sure you understand. That's a big part of their job.

The search for the best idea among myriad possibilities is a journey creatives must be willing to make.

MATTHEW BARBER

WRITER, BARKER/DZP (NEW YORK, NEW YORK)

While growing up, Matt Barber was sent to church five times a week. He wasn't particularly evil or anything, his parents just seemed to think that much churching was about right. All that time spent in the pews gave Barber ample time to daydream and exercise his creativity—building a rich fantasy life for himself that may have startled his pastor.

Today, Barber is a writer at Barker/DZP, a creative boutique in SoHo that lists the History Channel, Major League Soccer and the G4 network among its clients. He previously worked at StrawberryFrog (also in New York City) and worked on Microsoft, Heineken, Volvo and Manwich accounts.

When Matt Barber is not wordsmithing ads, he's writing short stories and scripts and telling well-crafted jokes at parties.

aciphex
omeprazole
protonix
zegerid
prevacid solutabs

I'm not sure whose bright idea it was to start tearing down agency walls, but I hate him.

Process

"Process? That's funny. I work in a large room with about twenty other people, and distractions abound. Between meetings at the big table in front of me, meetings at the art director's desk to the left of me, meetings at the art director's desk behind me, impromptu water-cooler-type conversations to the right of me, loud bellowing over beers in the kitchen, the editor cutting something with the volume on eleven, somebody doing something smelly in the bathroom a few feet from my desk, and some pissed off co-worker just walking around and mumbling under his breath, it's amazing I get anything done. I'm not sure whose bright idea it was to start tearing down agency walls, but I hate him. I mean, most writers describe putting words on the page as a solitary endeavor, so how did we get to a place where copywriters are sitting in a room full of people? I'd do anything for an office: just a place to shut out the noise and have a little quiet so I can hear the writer in my head.

"That being said, I think one of the most important keys to being creative is just to be available. Inspiration can be a slippery thing; even the ancient Greeks knew the Muses were bitches. So when it comes, I try to seize it. To have the pen and paper ready. To catch whatever's coming before it turns foul. It may mean long hours, a lot of coffee, more acetaminophen and even more prescription strength antacids, but when something comes together that you can really be proud of, it's all worth it."

—Matt Barber

Partner

"Matt and I were hired together as a junior team at StrawberryFrog right out of school. If you asked me then about his creative process, I'd have probably shrugged my shoulders a bit. But now that I've worked with a couple of other writers, I can look back and recognize the unique ways Matt thinks.

"I would describe Matt as a purveyor of culture. Matt watches more movies than anyone I know. He reads more books. And he's a copywriter who loves art, which was always fun for me. He's always seeking out new things. He once asked me to teach him some things in Photoshop. Then he Photoshopped mustaches on pictures of me for the next twenty minutes.

"Matt liked introducing new things to me. He would check out books for me at the library near his apartment in Brooklyn. On Fridays in the summer, Matt would be the first to say, 'Hey, let's go to a museum.' I remember Matt and I went to the Museum of Modern Art one afternoon and everything we saw reminded us of a vagina or a penis. (If you know Matt, you know he has a very fun, twisted sense of humor.) Overall, it was Matt's constant consumption of culture that really brought a lot to the way we worked. If we were ever stuck during a brainstorm, we always had a ton of things to talk about until the ideas starting kicking in again."

—Laura LeBel, Art Director, Mendelsohn Zien, Los Angeles

INSIGHTS FROM THE PROCESS CANVAS

Being creative for a living can amount to a Faustian bargain. You're hired to be brilliant and to deliver what's new and fresh every day, all day long. You figure out how to keep going and try not to self-destruct somewhere along the way.

There's something about caffeine and creativity. Art directors and writers consume enough energy drinks, sodas and espressos to keep those product categories profitable.

Here's a writer with an artistic eye. There are more of them out there than most art directors might want to admit.

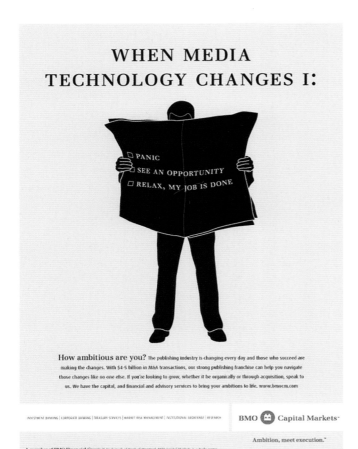

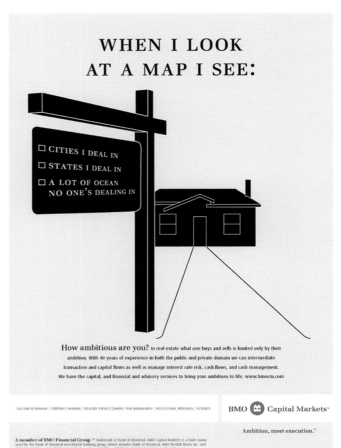

≫ ≪ BMO CAPITAL MARKETS MAGAZINE ADS

Tagline: Ambition, meet execution. **Agency:** StrawberryFrog, New York **Chief Creative Officer:** Scott Goodson **Executive Creative Director:** Kevin McKeon **Creative Director:** Brian Platt **Creative Director/Art Director:** Tricia Ting **Writer:** Matthew Barber **Client:** Bank of Montreal

ROSS CHOWLES

CO-FOUNDER/EXECUTIVE CREATIVE DIRECTOR, THE JUPITER DRAWING ROOM (CAPE TOWN, SOUTH AFRICA)

Ross Chowles leads young creative Samita Brinjal through a critique in TJDR offices.

Young creatives of the world, take note: There is a world outside New York City. Across the globe, at a beautiful shop in Cape Town, South Africa, you'll find a terrific advocate for good work: Ross Chowles.

Chowles based much of his professional career on creating smart design and building new agency models and, in the process, became an expert manager of creative talent. He shares his passion for advertising easily. He fantasizes about being a teacher (someone should tell him he's been teaching for a while now). Witness "The Ripple Effect," an educational initiative for young students he launched in 2004, as well as the successful juniors he has coached through his three-decade career. Or consider his annual trek to The One Show Workshops in Beijing and Shanghai where he enlightens hundreds of Chinese students about the business. Chowles loves the way students and newly minted professionals

The creative process

Receive the brief.
Absorb the information about the problem/product/target market.

__Just__ listen.
Listening is the **MOST** important part of creativity. Whether it's listening to the client or the consumer.

Just listen

②

Then just live with it.
Don't do anything.
Don't think of solutions.

JUST WALLOW
LIE IN THE INFORMATION
Let it sit with you.
Let it itch. Don't scratch.

③

When the ideas come, let them all out.

Don't censor your ideas. Big, small, silly or boring. Get them all out.

④

Pick your favorites using three criteria:
1. Relevance to product/consumer
2. Impact. Will people talk about your idea
3. What is the feeling/message the consumer will be left with after seeing your idea.

[2 | 1 | 3]

Pick your favorite

⑤

Once you have your idea, hang on to it.
People will try (not on purpose) fuck up your idea. They will chisel away at it with tiny little chips, till it looks nothing like the idea you started with. Hang on to good advice. Discard the bad.

think, and he loves the creative spirit of people still eager to learn.

Chowles has judged shows in France (Cannes Lions), New York (The One Show, the Art Directors Club of New York, the Clios), Canada and even Namibia. He has also won his fair share of awards around the globe. As executive creative director and co-founder of The Jupiter Drawing Room, he is the force behind the most awarded independent agency in Africa. "South Africa is the collision of cultures, the tension between the past and the future," he wrote on a recent African design blog. "This creates an environment of energy, the perfect energy for creative thinking."

Even with his heralded career and international influence, what his colleagues and friends often comment about first is Chowles's giving nature. "Ross is a talented painter," says Kevin Swanepoel, president of The One Club for Art & Copy in New York. "He paints beautiful portraits of people who have touched his life."

Process

"The part I love in the process is when you crack the idea and suddenly all of the possibilities come flooding forward, unfolding, growing. It's like a mental orgasm mixed with a sense of relief."

—Ross Chowles

Partner

"There are two defining features of Ross Chowles's creative process that his drawing accurately reflects.

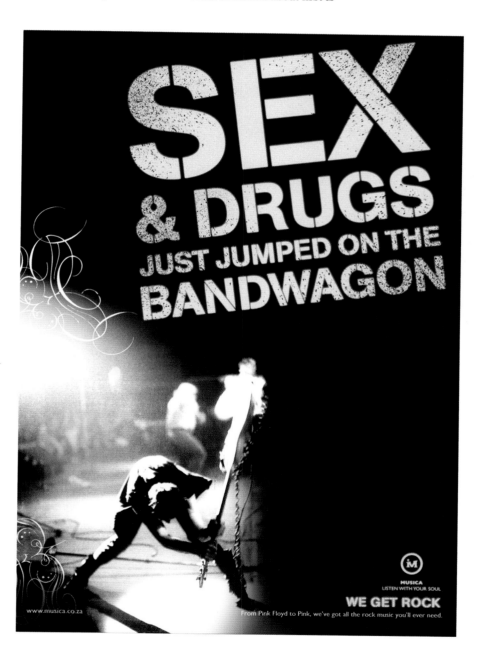

《 ☆ "WE GET ROCK" POSTERS

Agency: The Jupiter Drawing Room, Cape Town, South Africa **Executive Creative Director:** Ross Chowles **Creative Director:** Darren McKay **Art Director:** Ashraf Majiet **Writer:** Sanjiv Mistry **Client:** Musica

"The first is that Ross's process is dead simple; just about as uncomplicated as he is. That means no fancy modeling or complex intellectualizations. And the implication is that ideas can come from anyone. Everybody is welcome to join in and everybody does. No hierarchy, no exclusivity, no over-the-top creative egos.

"The second is that his process borrows on the most human of activities; like listening and wallowing and vomiting. And this is relevant because it is everyday life in all of its messiness which Ross draws on as his inspiration. It means that each of his ideas carries a little piece of Ross hidden at its heart. But more importantly, because ideas that are based on real life make for work that speaks to the human in all of us, Ross creates work that touches hearts.

"What this representation fails to show is the laughter that fills all the space in between. More than anything, working with Ross is fun: laughing as much at each other as we do at ourselves!"

—Claire Cobbledick, Deputy Managing
Director, The Jupiter Drawing Room

INSIGHTS FROM THE PROCESS CANVAS

The belief that a good idea will come can sustain you. Try to enjoy the wait.

Do more listening than talking and you'll get smarter, faster. Just listen.

Tenacity is a continuous thread here. This guy has perseverance and confidence.

« "KINGS OF THE COURT" POSTER

Agency: The Jupiter Drawing Room, Cape Town, South Africa **Executive Creative Director:** Ross Chowles **Art Director:** PJ Kensley **Writer:** Ahmed Tilly **Client:** Mentos

TOM CHRISTMANN

CREATIVE DIRECTOR, JWT (NEW YORK, NEW YORK)

Tom Christmann's passion for social media combined with his ability to find the big idea and tell a brand story have led him to work at some of the best agencies in New York, most recently as a creative director on Microsoft at JWT. He also once rode an elevator alone with David Ogilvy. Yes, that David Ogilvy.

Prior to working at JWT, Tom was executive creative director at Cliff Freeman & Partners, where he helped to bring Cliff Freeman's unique brand of impactful storytelling into the twenty-first century on brands like Quiznos and Baskin-Robbins. And he helped create a snazzy new website for an agency that wasn't known for its digital chops.

Christmann also worked at Taxi in New York. As creative director there, he helped build entirely new integrated campaigns for Amp'd Mobile, Blue Shield of California, Molson Canadian beer and the Versus television network.

feed://feeds.copyblogger.com/Copyblogger

http://adage.com/digitalnext/

http://threeminds.organic.com/

http://fffff.at/

http://www.thewebissocial.com/

http://fuelingnewbusiness.com/

http://knowmediablog.com/

http://www.barbariangroup.com/posts

http://news.cnet.com/

http://sethgodin.typepad.com/

http://searchengineland.com/

http://searchenginewatch.com/

http://makinads.blogspot.com/

http://www.chrisbrogan.com/

http://adrants.com/

http://www.micropersuasion.com/

http://www.psfk.com/

http://www.problogger.net/

http://adsoftheworld.com/

http://edwardboches.com

http://www.briansolis.com/

http://blogs.forrester.com/groundswell/

http://fivewords.mckinney.com/

http://www.thefwa.com/

http://bmorrissey.typepad.com/brianmorrissey/

http://mashable.com/

http://www.techcrunch.com/

+ <u>Real Life</u>*

* Real Life consists of some or all of the following: posters i've seen, movies, jokes, funny faces, emails, albums from the mid-seventies, funny-shaped pools of vomit on seventh avenue, horse poop, things my kids watch on television, ironic stories told by cabbies, stupid powerpoint graphs, trivial pursuit answers, cans of baked beans, clowns,

etc.
etc.
etc.

Ideas do not come out of thin air. Ideas only come out of combining other ideas. So the secret to coming up with ideas is to learn about lots of stuff.

As a creative director at BBDO in New York, Christmann was lucky enough to work directly with some of advertising's biggest names, including David Lubars and Eric Silver, and on some of the world's biggest brands—FedEx, eBay, Guinness, Red Stripe and AOL, to name a few. Christmann credits his six years at Kirshenbaum Bond & Partners in New York—as well as his first job at Ogilvy & Mather Direct—with giving him an appreciation for proven results and new technologies.

Christmann's work has been awarded Cannes Lions, One Show Pencils, ANDYs, ADDYs, Effies, Clios and an FWA (Favourite Website Award). He's also training to become a Lexulous champion on Facebook.

Process

"I submit that there is no such thing as imagination. At least not the way that most people think of it: the ability to come up with ideas and stories out of thin air, making stuff up. But I think that the human brain cannot make up something it's never seen or experienced or learned about. Ideas do not come out of thin air. Ideas only come out of combining other ideas. So the secret to coming up with ideas is to learn about lots of stuff. The more you know, the more you can combine and juxtapose. And people will think you have an amazing imagination. But you'll know better."

—Tom Christmann

Partner

"Tom and I began working together at Taxi, New York, several years ago. At the time, we met on our mutual first days on the job. We quickly became a solid team and worked on everything from Amp'd Mobile to Blue Shield to the Versus TV network to numerous successful new business pitches including Molson Canadian. We're both comfortable developing traditional and nontraditional ideas—whatever feels right for the brand and strategy—and we produced a bunch of work I'm proud of. He's a true writer in that you can sit in a room with him blurting out ideas back and forth, take off for a bit and come back, and not only is everything funnier than you thought it could be, it also sounds smarter and makes a hell of a lot more sense. Ideas only get better in Tom's hands.

"One thing that makes Tom such a great partner is that he's an old school idea guy. Tom never just comes up with one good idea and then calls it a day. He generates and generates and generates great concepts. Tom truly believes that ideas are not precious. And unlike some writers, Tom is a true craftsman. He really gets how an awkward pause here and there or an observational feeling wide shot instead of some cool camera angle can allow a funny idea to become even funnier as well as how his choice of words can convey the right emotion. It was a lot of fun to work together, not only on having an idea but on figuring out the best way to tell it. In this incredibly demanding business, it's easy to become stressed, but we'd grab a beer, relax and keep at it."

—Scott Bassen, Creative Director/
Art Director, JWT

INSIGHTS FROM THE PROCESS CANVAS

A list of websites constitutes a reservoir of cultural capital used for inspiration and (let's be honest) much-needed distraction.

The word "advertising" doesn't appear in the "real life" list. An abiding love for the business doesn't mean there can't be some space for horse poop.

IAN COHEN

CO-FOUNDER/CREATIVE DIRECTOR, WEXLEY SCHOOL FOR GIRLS (SEATTLE, WASHINGTON)

Wexley School for Girls co-owners/creative directors Cal McAllister and Ian Cohen on the shore of Puget Sound.

What are we to think about the irreverence of these Wexley characters? First, after dynamite stints at Hammerquist & Saffel in Seattle and Wieden+ Kennedy in Portland, Oregon, working on brands like Nike and K2, Ian Cohen (with creative partner Cal McAllister) had the nerve to start an agency that really doesn't sound like an agency. Then, he billed the place as an agency that is media neutral, singing their pitches to clients and using fart jokes like hammers, doing advertising that nobody thought of as advertising (362-degree introverted bipolar branding?). As it turned out, that's how a new little agency got featured in *Inc.* magazine.

It's obvious Ian Cohen likes this game. He went to school in North Carolina, loves his family and basketball, wears crazy T-shirts in the office and holds office meetings at picnic tables. In his spare time, he judges international award shows and speaks to advertising students around the country.

1. Input

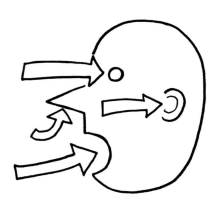

2. Blend

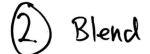

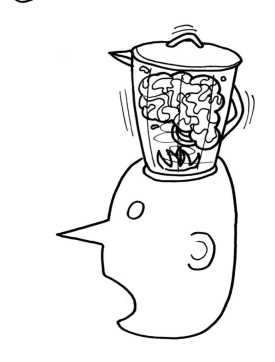

3. Tickle

4. Output

I like to pretend that I'm not at work so that any thinking doesn't seem work-related.

Cohen and McAllister lead a merry band working for Microsoft, Copper Mountain Ski Resort, Hyper-V Server, Brooks Sports and Pepsi, among other clients. They carve out smart little projects, take viral marketing where it should go and solve serious business problems in comedic and unexpected ways. As one Wexley team member explains: "You have to be really smart to have this kind of fun and make it work. That's Ian."

Process

"As far as thinking goes, I usually don't have to clear my head too much because it's already fairly empty. I just have to move the Duke basketball thoughts over to the side a little. There are several ways I think. I like to pretend that I'm not at work so that any thinking doesn't seem work-related. Additionally, I like to do my thinking in stimulating places, not my office. I like having motion, distractions and things to look at to spur on thought fragments.

"When I'm concepting for advertising, I need to know my target inside and out; then, my thinking turns into more of a conversation. Depending on the subject, I like to know what other work has been done in that arena, so I can mentally start in a totally different place. Maybe I have ADD, but I like to get a paper pad, a really cheap pad, that I can rifle through and write down anything that comes to mind in a free-flow stream of consciousness. I like to doodle, draw out thoughts and write out half sentences. And, the perfect pen is a must. I am always surprised at the end of one of my 'thought storms' how poorly I draw. Seriously, I can't even doodle an animal that resembles any real animal. After I know all I can know about a subject and I've free-flowed for a while, I'll come back to my favorite ideas and start to round them out and see if they are really good ideas or just farticles that I thought were good at the time."

—Ian Cohen

>> **"SCARF SEATTLE" CAMPAIGN**

Agency: Wexley School for Girls, Seattle
Creative Directors: Ian Cohen, Cal McAllister
Writers: Kyle Cavanaugh, Ian Cohen
Art Director: Kristen Curtis **Client:** Seattle Sounders Football Club

Seattle Sounders FC ©2009

Partner

"Ian and I always end up in a similar place but take different paths to get there. He's a tactical heavyweight fighter. He kind of studies something, toys with it a bit, starts talking about a really good eighth-grade basketball player who might commit to Duke and then BLAM out of nowhere an uppercut of hilarity or of creativity that you didn't see coming. He never surprises me by getting there, because he always gets there. Then he sits back, laughs a little bit, and BLAM another shot just so you don't think the first one was a lucky punch."

—Cal McAllister, Co-Founder/Creative
Director, Wexley School for Girls

INSIGHTS FROM THE PROCESS CANVAS

Joy, play and the fun of collaboration. Can you tickle yourself? Sure you can.

There's something dynamic, active—even violent—in the imagery here. Wrestling with your own thoughts can feel traumatic, leading to great catharsis when it's over.

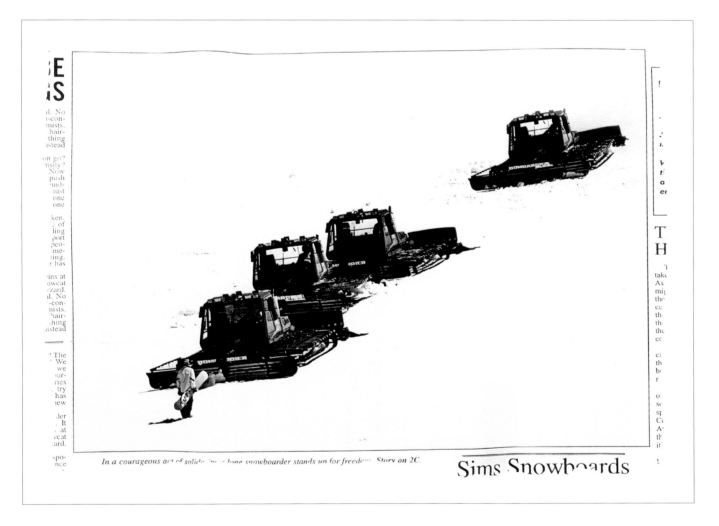

In a courageous act of solid... ...lone snowboarder stands up for freedom... Story on 2C.

Sims Snowboards

∧ "TIANANMEN" MAGAZINE AD

Copy: In a courageous act of solidarity, a lone snowboarder stands up for freedom.
– Story on 2C. **Agency:** Hammerquist & Saffel, Seattle **Creative Director:** Fred Hammerquist
Art Directors: Matt Peterson, Mike Proctor
Writer: Ian Cohen **Client:** Sims Snowboards

GLENN COLE

CO-FOUNDER/CREATIVE DIRECTOR, 72ANDSUNNY (SANTA MONICA, CALIFORNIA)

Glenn Cole began at the top. He graduated from the Honors College and the School of Journalism and Communication at the University of Oregon in the early 1990s, and promptly landed an internship at Wieden+Kennedy in Portland, Oregon, an agency where advertising is done right, with enduring craftsmanship and a flair for the iconic.

Cole got his start working on Nike, ESPN and the Oregon Tourism Board. Over a seven-year span at W+K's Amsterdam office, he served as creative director for Nike's European business unit. Along the way, he helped Nike grow from the fifth-largest global soccer brand in 1995 to number one in 2002.

Then he and art director partner John Boiler made a big jump of their own. Their agency, 72andSunny, is that independent, feisty shop that behaves like one of the big boys, doing work for international brands while keeping everything nimble and smart.

Cole is a member of The One Club board of directors and was named the inaugural Eric Allen Award recipient at the University of Oregon for alumni under forty years old who have made it big.

Process

"They say that great interviews are the result of great questions. But when it comes to my creative process, it's more like

QUESTION EVERYTHING.

I question how we could do it better next time, I question all of it.

an interrogation. I question the brief, I question my own solutions, I question our presentation, I question proposed channels, I question production methods, I question schedules, I question feedback, I question how we could do it better next time, I question all of it.

"Frankly, it is exhausting. And more than one of my partners has complained about it. Rightfully so. But in my experience, if you assume to know what's under every stone, you stop turning them over and you reduce the chance of being surprised. Plus, being a craftsman requires an intimate understanding of how things are made, whether it's an ad, an app, an experience or a brand.

"So, rather than focus on 'being creative,' I focus on challenging assumptions and asking the right questions. Creative solutions usually present themselves. Which is probably why the first, and arguably most important, question on any creative brief at 72andSunny is: 'What is the real problem we're trying to solve here?'"

—Glenn Cole

Partner

"Pablo Picasso said, 'Every act of creation is first an act of destruction.'

"And the Hindus say that life in this world is a manifestation of the three principles of creation, sustenance and destruction. And that apparent destruction is only an essential forerunner to creation.

"And to that, Glenn Cole might say: 'Really? You sure about that?'

"That's his thing. Before there can be creation, before there can be destruction, it all seems to start with a question for Glenn. A mental poke. 'How solid is your philosophical footing there, Picasso?' 'Is there any substance under your theology, Mr. Hindu?' Glenn isn't afraid to wonder and ask out loud. Get to the root of the idea and see if it's based on some fundamental

truth. Or at least on some really entertaining bullshit. That counts too.

"So, it's been my pleasure to work, question and destroy alongside Glenn for the past sixteen years. And it has been a very fulfilling and destructive time. I remember one creative director at Wieden+Kennedy, where Glenn had begun work as an intern, likening Glenn's creative process to a chainsaw. I think it was Larry Frey. He always had a way with metaphor. Anyhow, if you're from the Northwest, you know that some amazing and unlikely things can be made with chainsaws. Ten-foot-tall Douglas fir grizzly bear/Sasquatch/gnome totems for one. Patchwork quilt forest landscapes you can see from space for another. Powerful tool, the chainsaw. Fierce, gnawing and relentless. Like good questions.

"But it takes more than critical scrutiny to make anything good. And Glenn brings the rest by staying tapped into culture. Staying curious. And of course, by creating the connections between things, people and ideas that other people just don't see yet.

"Maybe that's the process. Violent deconstruction of things. Followed by unlikely re-assembly. All in a cloud of woodchips and oily blue smoke."

—John Boiler, Co-Founder/Creative Director, 72andSunny

INSIGHTS FROM THE PROCESS CANVAS

There's no BS, no trappings, no gilding the lily here. This minimalist statement is signaling what's most important in his process.

This couple of words against a wall of white space transmits intensity and conviction.

The World is Just Awesome

Discovery
CHANNEL

≈ "I LOVE THE WORLD" TV SPOT

Agency: 72andSunny, Los Angeles
Creative Director/Art Director: John Boiler
Creative Director/Writer: Glenn Cole
Client: Discovery Channel

©2009 Discovery Communications, LLC

« NBA 2K9 "THE OTHER SEASON" WEBSITE

Agency: 72andSunny, Los Angeles **Creative Director/Art Director:** John Boiler **Creative Director/Writer:** Glenn Cole **Client:** 2K Sports

SILVER CUELLAR

SENIOR ART DIRECTOR, FIREHOUSE (DALLAS, TEXAS)

S ilver Cuellar's list of creative awards and honors is almost as long as his facial hair. This self-described "native Texan and full-blooded Mexican" began his career in Austin at McGarrah Jessee in 2003, where his work helped the agency win three new business pitches and doubled its size. While there, he worked on the Whataburger, Shiner Beer, Central Market and Frost Bank accounts and became the first creative in the shop's history to win a Clio.

Boston-based Mullen hired Cuellar in 2005, where he worked on XM Satellite Radio, the Grain Foods Foundation and Four Seasons accounts, among others. *Lürzer's Archive* magazine featured his work and he won numerous Hatch Awards from the Ad Club of Boston. Despite his success, Cuellar missed Texas and—more specifically—the brisket.

In 2006, Cuellar moved to Dallas, where he joined the Richards Group as senior art director. One of the first campaigns he developed there, for Henk's European Deli & Black Forest Bakery, was featured in the *Communication Arts 2007 Advertising Annual.* His clients also included Chick-fil-A and Fruit of the Loom. In 2007, he joined TM Advertising and led teams working on the Nationwide Insurance and American Airlines business. A short film he created while at TM was selected by The One Show's One Screen Film Festival. Cuellar joined Dallas-based Firehouse in 2009.

Oh, and his prized collection of He-Man action figures? You can't play with them.

Process

"Approach each assignment like you have only one chance to show how you think. No matter the budget. No matter the key points of communication. No matter the mandatories, price offers or small legal copy. Don't compromise until you've got something that satisfies you. Sell something later.

"Do it for yourself first. It will directly reflect your ability as an ideator, your craft as an art director and your strategic thinking. It will keep all of those much-needed instruments in your head sharpened.

"Achieving this doesn't necessarily equate to one-hundred-hour workweeks. Staying until eleven P.M., going through hundreds of ideas, turning things around every time on seemingly impossible deadlines. That isn't hard to do. That can be done. But in the end, your work, your product, your output, will ultimately reflect that. That's foolish. People and agencies who demand that from you are more the fools for demanding it, let alone expecting it. Be smart enough not to compromise your balance between life and office.

"Know that each time an AE [account executive] rounds the corner of your cube, you have the chance to add to your portfolio. By doing that, you can stand by every piece in your book and know it's a piece that not only can get you hired, but can also show off your brain. Careers can live and die on that.

⌃ SHINER BEER BILLBOARDS

Agency: McGarrah Jessee, Austin, Texas
Art Directors/Writers: Silver Cuellar, Craig Crutchfield, Derrit DeRouen **Client:** Shiner Beers

"I heard the other day that there is too much filler in student books. There shouldn't be any filler in any portfolio, professional or student. If you create work knowing the end result may be your only shot at showing how you think, you won't need stronger work to save your weaker work. It will all be strong.

"Your process will make this happen. It will force it to happen. This standard makes your work, your book, and the process rewarding each time. It is the absolute reflection of your mind on a page.

"That's your greatest commodity. That's your brand."

—Silver Cuellar

Partner

"I think Silver is just fearless. He's one of those guys who is smart enough to stay on strategy but also wise enough to know that if you stay totally on strategy your ad will suck. Plus it's nice to work with people who will show a creative director or client work they truly believe is the best, regardless of the brief or budget.

"He also has mad illustrating skills. I know that's not totally key to the process, but most art directors only know how to draw a circle, maybe a square or some stick figures. When you can draw like Silver, it makes the process faster, your comps look better, and your work will communicate better and have a better chance of selling through.

"Silver also keeps the ideas going. If you've ever concepted with someone, you know there is a point where the talking stops and you just sit silently and stare at each other for a few minutes. Maybe ten minutes. You start staring off into space and it's hard to pull yourself back into a good thinking session. But some people know how to get it going again. Silver is one of them.

"Oh, one more thing—a huge thing: Silver is forever a student of the game. Ask him about any ad Carmichael Lynch did for Porsche in the last ten years. He'll know."

—Brooks Jackson, Writer, Goodby,
Silverstein & Partners, San Francisco

INSIGHTS FROM THE PROCESS CANVAS

It makes sense that we strongly, personally identify with everything we create. It's part of who we are. That's why criticism is sometimes hard to take.

The best art directors revel in detail. They notice everything and can see flaws invisible to most. They find (and can show us) beauty in unexpected places.

⌃ "FROM HOLLAND/FROM HELL" MAGAZINE AD

Headline: Family recipes from Holland. Accordion solos from Hell. **Tagline:** A little bit of Amsterdam in Dallas. **Agency:** The Richards Group, Dallas **Art Director:** Silver Cuellar **Writer:** Brian Dunaway **Client:** Henk's European Deli & Black Forest Bakery

Henk's European Deli, Inc. ©2009

HAL CURTIS

CREATIVE DIRECTOR, WIEDEN+KENNEDY (PORTLAND, OREGON)

Wieden+
Kennedy

Hal Curtis is an award-winning creative director for some of the biggest brands in the world. (Maybe you've heard of Coca-Cola and Nike?) He's won awards from D&AD, the Art Directors Club, The One Show and Cannes Lions. The Museum of Modern Art, *Communication Arts* and *Graphis* have featured his work. He's also a two-time Emmy winner. But in 2008, he did something no one has ever done before: He made Charlie Brown a winner.

Curtis's Super Bowl spot for Coca-Cola, titled "It's Mine," is set at Macy's Thanksgiving Day Parade and features giant balloons in the likenesses of Underdog, Stewie Griffin from *Family Guy* and everyone's favorite loser, Charlie Brown. The three characters break free from their handlers and chase a giant Coca-Cola balloon across the New York City skyline. In a surprise twist, the hapless Charlie Brown outsmarts the competition and captures the prize. The spot was a favorite

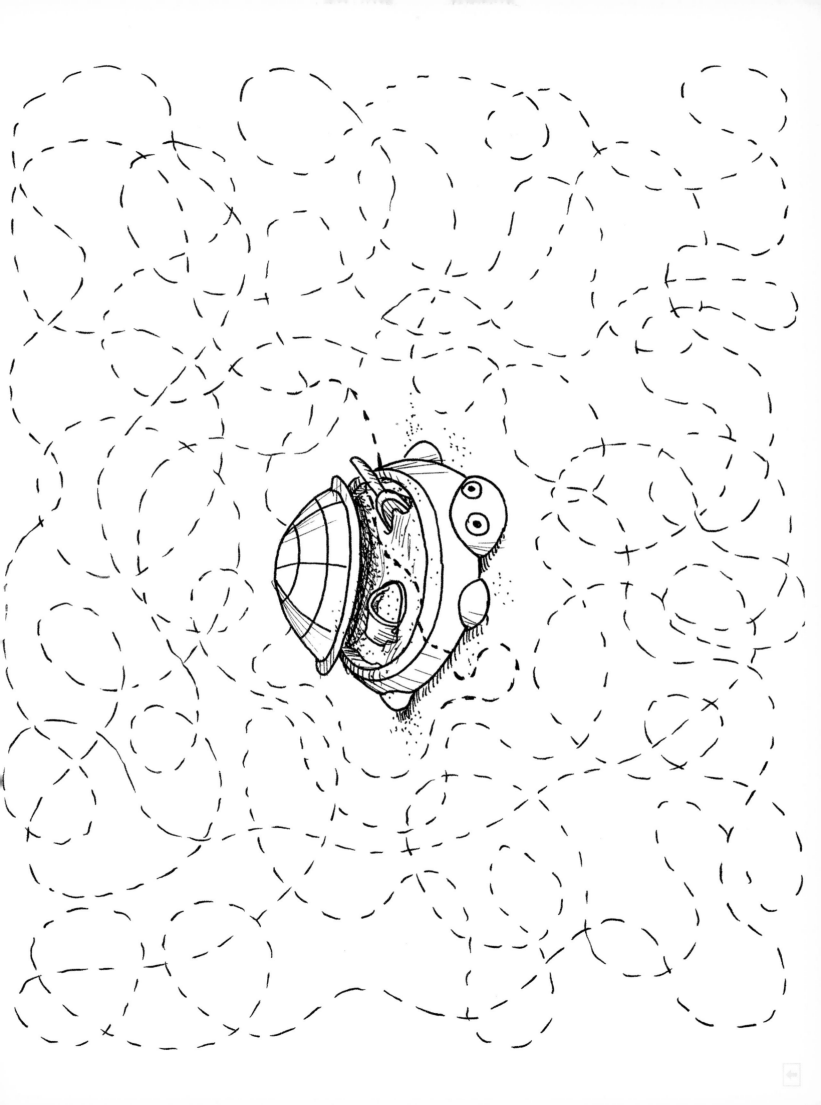

In every assignment, there is a small space where you, the agency, the client and the consumer can be happy.

of critics and viewers alike and is considered one of the best commercials in Super Bowl history.

A native Texan, Curtis started at Wieden+Kennedy in 1994. In 2006, *Advertising Age* named him one of the fifty most influential creative leaders of the last twenty years.

Process

"In every assignment, there is a small space where you, the agency, the client and the consumer can be happy. I call it a sandbox. Find it—it takes good judgment, patience and intuition. And once you do, create excellence within it."

—Hal Curtis

Partner

"Hal Curtis is quiet.

"Working with Hal Curtis is quiet.

"Hal is quiet, quiet and quiet until he says, 'What if we did this?'

"Then we do his 'this.'

"And it works.

"Then Hal goes back to being quiet until the next time he says, 'What if we did this?'"

—Jim Riswold, Artist and former
Creative Director, Wieden+Kennedy

INSIGHTS FROM THE PROCESS CANVAS

Insight: The sandbox communicates play. And they are always more fun with playmates.

Insight: Ideas are a little like sandcastles. They can be beautiful, but they're fragile. It isn't wise to get too attached.

 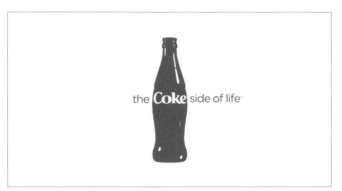

≈ "IT'S MINE" TV SPOT

Agency: Wieden+Kennedy, Portland, Oregon
Creative Directors: Hal Curtis, Sheena Brady
Art Director: Hal Curtis **Writer:** Sheena Brady
Client: Coca-Cola

PEANUTS © United Feature Syndicate, Inc.

Family Guy™ ©2009 Twentieth Century Fox Film
Corporation. All rights reserved.

The Underdog character is owned by Classic Media, Inc.
and used with permission.

GREG EIDEN

FREELANCE WRITER/CREATIVE DIRECTOR (PORTLAND, OREGON)

Living the Portland, Oregon, life means that you will necessarily become expert in a few appropriate areas: outdoor adventure, good beer and the environment. Greg Eiden—author of books and award-winning advertising—is a Portlander through and through.

Eiden fled the Minneapolis Metropolitan Mosquito Control District in the 1980s to join Borders, Perrin & Norrander in Portland. After ten years of fun work for Columbia Sportswear and Portland General Electric—including One Show Pencils, features in *Communication Arts* and other honors—he left to co-found Sasquatch Advertising. At Sasquatch, the client roster included Leatherman tools, CamelBak and Widmer Brothers Brewing, among other lucky Northwestern brands. The spirited lyrical work he and his creative team produced is legendary in the region.

He's a freelance writer now, as well as the author (along with graphic artist Kurt D. Hollomon) of the books *Northwest Basic Training: Essential Skills for Visitors, Newcomers & Native Northwesterners*, and *In Gear: A Bike Journal*. He's taught at the School of Journalism and Communication at the University of Oregon, inspiring a young crop of writers to explore their adventurous side. Eiden continues to find the spirit of the Northwest an essential part of his writer's life.

Process

"The creative product, the conception of an idea, is very much about the creative struggle.

"An ongoing, relentless, exhausting and exhilarating process, I find it is often as much about what you do away from the computer as what you do on it. Step out to visit a museum. Walk the dog. Take a nap. Or, perhaps best of all, take in a

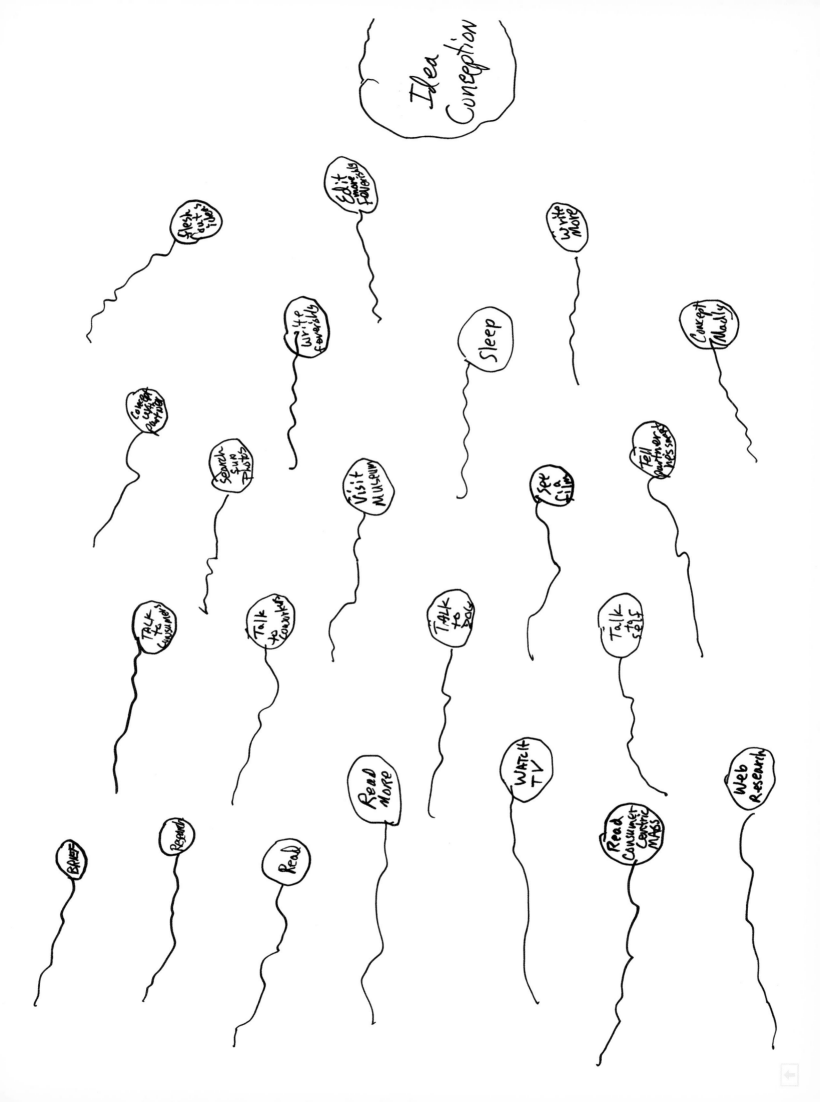

The creative product, the conception of an idea, is very much about the creative struggle.

baseball game. Those moments often give birth to the best ideas."

—Greg Eiden

Partner

"Greg and I have been creative partners for almost twenty years. Over that span, together we've come up with thousands of concepts. Some good, some not so good.

"Greg's brain and thought process, like many others, is heavily influenced by pop culture, news of the day, current events and art, to name a few. It's rare when you don't find him in a bookstore. The guy reads everything.

"Greg's typical problem-solving approach goes something like this:

Reads creative brief, sets it aside.

Meets art director at a bookstore.

Talks/concepts while thumbing through stacks of magazines totally unrelated to the assignment, all the while taking notes.

Divorces self from thinking directly about the project for a bit. (In reality, the guy never stops thinking.)

Meets art director again at bookstore (or this time maybe a bar) to share ideas.

Rolls eyes at art director's dumb ideas.

Reassures and calms panicky art director.

Goes away and writes.

Meets art director for lunch. This time armed with what were once-random thoughts, senseless drivel, seedless germs of ideas and, yes, art director's dumb ideas, neatly organized in a ten-to-fifteen-page document that now makes sense. Adjourn to bookstore.

More concepting/whittling down ideas.

"After several sessions like this, we have magic."

—Tim Parker, Art Director, Portland, Oregon

INSIGHTS FROM THE PROCESS CANVAS

Among many sources of fertilization, which will take hold in the brain? Which will yield the new idea?

The creative process is organic and quite miraculous at its core.

Yes, sometimes sleep can be as nourishing to the brain as a trip to a museum.

☆ "TOOL TALES, NO. 6" MAGAZINE AD

Headline: We had two choices: crash in
Dillingham or head back to Anchorage and
crash there. **Tagline:** One tool. A couple
thousand uses. **Agency:** Sasquatch Advertising,
Portland, Oregon **Creative Director/Art
Director:** Tim Parker **Creative Director/Writer:**
Greg Eiden **Client:** Leatherman

DANNY GREGORY

MANAGING PARTNER/EXECUTIVE CREATIVE DIRECTOR, McGARRYBOWEN (NEW YORK, NEW YORK)

Andrea Scher, www.superherodesigns.com/journal ©2009

mcgarrybowen

Danny Gregory had an international childhood. He was born in London and lived there until the age of four. His family moved to Pittsburgh and then to Australia; then, at age nine, Gregory went to live with his grandparents in Pakistan. He remembers only one television commercial from those days, but it made such an impression on him that he still recalls every word, all sung in Urdu.

The spot was for Lipton Tea. Forty years later, Gregory still drinks Lipton Tea.

He's worked as an assistant at a slaughterhouse, and as an intern at the White House (he jokes that Jimmy Carter lusted for him only in his heart) and a half-dozen advertising agencies. Today, he's managing partner and executive creative director at mcgarrybowen in New York. He supervises the Chase account and has also worked on the *Wall Street Journal*, Crayola, Chevron and Verizon.

Gregory is also a fantastic illustrator trapped in the body of a copywriter. It shouldn't surprise anyone, therefore, that he's a believer in the power of artistic expression. He's written several books on the topic, including *Everyday Matters*, *The Creative License* and *An Illustrated Life*. Having led a life filled with fascinating and unusual experiences, he is a true Renaissance man.

Process

"I am pretty good at coming up with ideas quickly—lots of them—some good, most bad. There are several reasons for this facility.

"First is practice: I've been a creative director for a while now. All that experience has given me confidence in my ability to come up with answers and helps stifle the Critic until I need him. My advice: Work on as many projects as possible, develop as many ideas as possible. Wait to polish until you have a rich pile of nuggets.

"Second is raw material: I have always been a voracious dabbler, and I am constantly looking for new sources of inspiration. I rarely read advertising trades or award annuals, but prefer to see what illustrators, street artists, independent filmmakers, small bands and graphic designers are up to. I visit my library every Saturday morning and return home with a half-dozen books (fiction and nonfiction, bios, how-to, history, art, experimental, pulp, etc.) and a dozen DVDs. I go to concerts, museums, galleries, dance performances, clubs, Broadway, opera, experimental theater, puppet shows and street performances. I listen to a lot of podcasts, from NPR, the TED [Technology, Entertainment, Design] conference, and various universities. All of this input can be useful as direct reference; I have it at my fingertips, fresh in my brain, ready to be pulled up and adapted, combined, and reformed into a fresh idea.

"Third is space: Not my office or studio, but mental distance and calm. I walk a lot, generally an hour or more a day, time in which I might listen to music or a podcast, but often just think, write in my head, kick ideas around. If something hits me, I scrawl it on a piece of paper or into my BlackBerry, then keep going. I also find that while I'm sleeping, my imagination is working on assignments. Sometimes I sit up at four A.M. with an idea (often only half-baked) and I tiptoe out to my desk and work on it a while, then e-mail it to myself.

"It's only when I have lots of ideas arrayed before me that I sharpen my knives and start to whittle them down to the very best."

—Danny Gregory

Partner

DG: "How about… ?"

HM: [And he's off again with visionary gymnastics—the pommel horse champion takes to the rings, following a perfect 10.0 on floor and high bar.]

DG: "What are you thinking?"

HM: "I'm thinking about breakfast; about a water bill my wife asked me to pay (three weeks ago); about my intention to leave early after arriving late. You know, ad man stuff. Shall we get a coffee?" [I hope my pleading isn't noticeable.]

DG: "Just tell me what you think first."

HM: "Oh God, why first? Why not second? Mañana, man. Slow down."

DG: "Ah!" [He says; I jump.] "Take a look at this… "

HM: [I grip the sides of my seat as the ride takes off. Oh no, what's this? He's written a strategy, searched out diverse video footage, spliced it together, found the right music, added his own voice-over, timed the whole thing and hand drawn the logo mnemonic. I'm wondering if he's already bought the airtime.

How is he doing it? More importantly, how is he doing it so early? He's clever of course—a Princeton man—but hell, my university has status, too. The difference is, I didn't finish, and by all accounts his thesis was dry by lunchtime. Why doesn't that surprise me? Nothing's changed. Already this morning he's thrust half a dozen ideas and I haven't parried, let alone touché-d.]

DG: "What do you think?"

HM: "What do I think? I think you're too smart, too fleet. Too cultured. Too inquisitive. Too interested in everything. Too interesting for Monday morning… for this business.

"I know the answer. He enjoys this. Throwing down the gauntlet, simultaneously raising the bar.

"My partner. Ads infinitum. Danny Gregory, ladies and gentlemen."

—Haydn Morris, Executive Creative Director,
mcgarrybowen, New York

INSIGHTS FROM THE PROCESS CANVAS

There's an appreciable certainty here about the nature of the creative process. Years of experience can bring a level of comfort and familiarity but doesn't have to spoil the fun.

Visuals and words work together to convey meaning. They can clarify and enrich each other. Great writers and art directors share this understanding.

 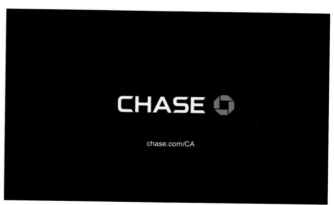

⌃ "BLUE SKY" TV SPOT

Agency: mcgarrybowen, New York **Executive Creative Director/Art Director:** Haydn Morris **Executive Creative Director/Writer:** Danny Gregory **Client:** Chase Banking

©2009 JPMorgan Chase Bank, N.A. Reprinted with permission. All rights reserved.

ANDY HALL

FREELANCE WRITER/CREATIVE DIRECTOR (NEW YORK, NEW YORK)

The list of clients Andy Hall handled as a New York agency veteran of more than a dozen years includes both the fashionable (Ray-Ban, Godiva, Calvin Klein, Bombay Sapphire, Cunard Cruise Line) and the functional (Domino's Pizza, IKEA and AT&T). Hall began his career as a writer at Young & Rubicam, where his big break came in the form of a national television spot for AT&T based on his sister's propensity for skidding off icy roads with small children in the car. He moved on to Deutsch, where his campaign for Domino's Pizza, featuring a fuzzy, mischievous creature and the tagline "Bad Andy. Good Pizza," won the account. *Adweek* recognized his work for IKEA as a "Best Spot" in 1998.

Hall left Deutsch to join TBWA\Chiat\Day's New York office in 2000, where he helped win the Cunard Cruise Line and A&E network business. A 2002 graduate of the Absolut Akademi in Åhus, Sweden, he wrote the launch campaigns for Absolut

Vanilia and Level Vodka, as well as the first long copy campaign for the brand, which was later featured in *Lürzer's Archive*.

In 2005, Hall was named associate creative director at Sugartown Creative, a new boutique agency launched by ad veteran Fritz Westenberger. There, he worked on Bombay Sapphire and helped win the Godiva, *Penthouse* magazine and David Barton Gym accounts. For Procter & Gamble, he named a new product, Swash, and helped bring it to a laundry-adverse college market. Since 2008, Hall has been freelancing at Kirshenbaum Bond + Partners working on HomeGoods, Cablevision and Wendy's. He is an avid traveler and tennis geek, and is working on his first novel.

Process

"I went to an Eames exhibit once and there was this cabinet of tiny drawers filled with all these different buttons that they

» **SELF-PROMOTIONAL T-SHIRT DESIGN**

Agency: Sugartown Creative, New York
Creative Director: Fritz Westenberger **Writer:**
Andy Hall **Designer:** Joel Luna **Client:**
Sugartown Creative

kept around for inspiration, size and shape reference, what-ever. It struck me that if I kept a cabinet like that, I'd never know where to look. It's the same with memories—they're all in there somewhere, the experiences and people and little stories. But where? Which drawer? I drew the fish analogy because it seems like when I manage to find the quiet space in my thoughts, inspiration will surface and find me. A lot of it isn't very useful, feelings and images that don't really trans-late into scripts and headlines. But as raw material, they can lead to ideas that have the right spirit for the project at hand."

—Andy Hall

Partner

"Andy pretends there's some sort of magic to his creative pro-cess, that once he gets an assignment, bits of information float-ing about the air on his coffee runs and bicycle rides home just start presenting themselves, and he throws it all in his top hat and pulls out a rabbit. Ha! I have proof that it's all a calculated physiological process.

"Once we found him in the exit stair vestibule standing on his head. He said he just got this wild hair to try to break the Guinness World Record, but upon Googling we saw that a man in India did it for fourteen days, and there was no way Andy was going to miss the Williams sisters playing in the U.S. Open semis, much less the free muffins the photo rep

was bringing later that day. So I knew he was trying to rush more type B to his cranium to corral all those 'fishy' ideas into one big bloodstream of consciousness. After three hours, he passed out, which wasn't pretty. When we revived him, his first words were 'anvil catapult' and he staggered to his sketchbook (yes he's a writer, but a writer who tries to draw is much less silly than an AD who tries to write). Anyway, he proceeded to draw up the brilliant idea that won us the Acme Gadgets pitch. Client marketing head Wile E. Coyote actu-ally stood up and clapped in the meeting. From that point on, whenever I needed some of Andy's creative juice, I gladly took him to the vestibule and held his feet up for three hours."

—Fritz Westenberger, Owner/Creative
Director, Hazelwood, New York

INSIGHTS FROM THE PROCESS CANVAS

Every creative project has a start and a finish, but the jour-ney between the two is the focus here. There is movement and convergence toward some destination.

The visual metaphor, the fish, communicates the life and energy that flourishes in relative silence, like an active brain in a quiet room.

JIM HAVEN

CO-FOUNDER/CREATIVE DIRECTOR, CREATURE (SEATTLE, WASHINGTON)

With fifteen years of copywriting experience in the creative enclaves of Portland, San Francisco, Seattle and Amsterdam, Jim Haven co-founded Creature in 2002 and serves as co-creative director of the agency. His role is to keep the Creature perspective on the work, and also to energize and enable the agency to think in new ways.

Working for the ad agencies Borders, Perrin & Norrander, Goodby, Silverstein & Partners and StrawberryFrog exposed Haven to virtually every brand category imaginable and contributed to an extensive client list. Over the years, he has lent his expertise and creativity to Pacifico Beer, Umpqua Bank, Palm, Google, Nike, Starbucks, Capgemini, HBO, the *Wall Street Journal*, E*Trade, Porsche, Isuzu, Sprint and more. His leadership in developing innovative campaigns has also garnered industry recognition in publications such as *Adweek*, *Advertising Age*, *Communication Arts*, *One. A Magazine*, *Shoot*, *Shots* and the *New York Times* have sought his input. Haven has been invited to speak at events around the world, including The One Club Workshop in Shanghai. He is also a member of Creative Social, an invitation-only group of international progressive and digital-focused creative leaders.

Not bad for a guy who, according to a 2005 interview with *Adweek*, is afraid of mayonnaise.

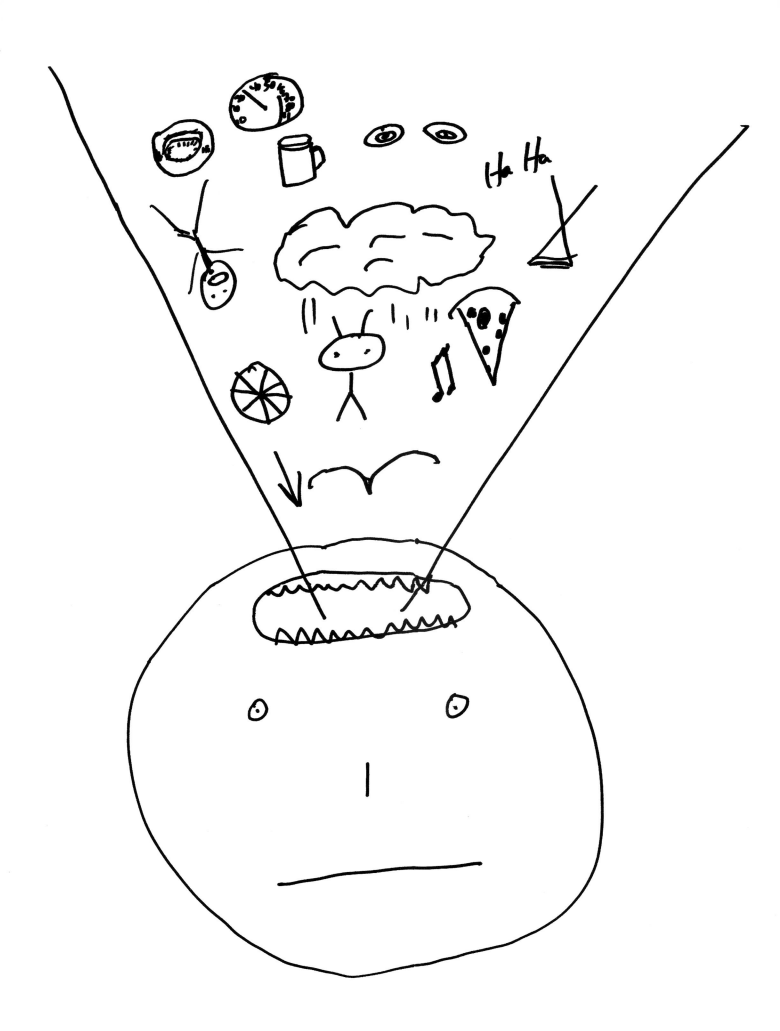

Process

"Creativity is rarely a linear process. If I knew how to channel my creativity on demand, life would be much easier and advertising would be a nine-to-five job and weekends would be just like you see in commercials. But, I do have a few personal theories. I feel that creativity usually happens on the side of your thoughts rather than the front or the back. It's a non-linear byproduct of thinking about something logically. You can't logic creativity. You really can't even make creativity. You can only hope to replicate the process in which creativity might develop, like a petri dish for your thoughts. To me, it's like flexing a muscle and relaxing. The relaxing is where the magic happens. Basically, I think or write furiously around a subject, not directly to it. Sometimes that subject is barely related to the problem I want to solve. And because I can't draw, the writing is often just a manifestation of visual thoughts. Then, in the middle of everything, I stop, get up to get a glass of water or something, and that's when my idea hits me. Over time, you get better at this process. And you don't physically have to move, you just need to switch your mind over to something else. Unfortunately, these switches usually come in the form of interruptions, which aren't quite the same.

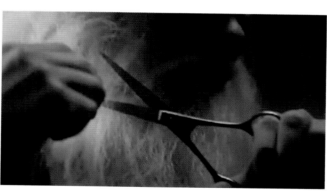

≲ "CLAÜS" TV SPOT

Agency: Creature, Seattle **Creative Directors:**
Jim Haven, Matt Peterson **Art Director:** Adam
Deer **Writers:** Peter Trueblood, Yutaka Tsujino
Client: Palm, Inc.

"Early on, I was stymied by fear, yet at the same time it fueled me. Now, I think efficiency is my greatest motivation. Both create a sense of urgency. And I think that's the secret ingredient. Finally, you need to be okay with putting lots of bad ideas out there in order to select a good idea from the rubble."

—Jim Haven

Partner

"My first encounter with Jim's unique view on the world was way back in college, when he left a message for my roommate on our answering machine. It was the lyrics to R.E.M.'s 'Losing My Religion' but the lyrics were changed to 'Losing My Burrito.' That song, to me, is forever now about pinto beans, too much filler rice and a missing burrito.

"Jim has always been about turning things on their head, always experimenting with improbable 'what ifs.' 'What if a hermit crab wanted a more modern home?' or, 'What if you could wake up to a live rooster crow from Mexico, on your computer?' When he gets excited about a new idea, he runs around the office sharing bits of it, gauging initial laughs and looking for people to add to the idea that has just been hatched. There are lots of these moments of spark. Jim doesn't have the longest attention span in the world, but it means the volume of new thoughts is always high.

"Jim has an unending drive to create the next great idea. He loves to make people laugh and join him on his often-bizarre scenarios, many of which lead to great advertising stories. Working with Jim is about constantly creating. He says he's in advertising because he couldn't actually do anything else. He's probably right, but his mind and gift for creating memorable stories that solve business problems couldn't be better suited for what we do here."

—Matt Peterson, Co-Founder/Creative Director, Creature

INSIGHTS FROM THE PROCESS CANVAS

The expressionless face here offers a reminder that the brain is always working, regardless of how we look on the outside.

Out of apparent chaos, the mind can synthesize, organize and bring order in the form of a creative solution to a problem.

⌃ "MEXICO VIA PACIFICO" BILLBOARD

Agency: Creature, Seattle **Creative Directors:** Jim Haven, Matt Peterson **Art Director:** Lara Papadakis **Writer:** Peter Trueblood **Client:** Pacifico Beer, Crown Imports, LLC

« "MEXICO VIA PACIFICO" MAGAZINE AD

Agency: Creature, Seattle **Creative Directors:** Jim Haven, Matt Peterson **Art Director:** Lara Papadakis **Writer:** Peter Trueblood **Client:** Pacifico Beer, Crown Imports, LLC

MIKE HEID

WRITER, PETER A. MAYER ADVERTISING (NEW ORLEANS, LOUISIANA)

As a graduate student, Mike Heid won a national Gold ADDY Award for a point-of-purchase display idea. He and a partner designed and built a giant, exact replica of an old-fashioned mousetrap for installation in grocery stores. The mousetrap was "baited" with boxes of cheese-flavored crackers and carried the tagline "Get Nipped." Here's a guy whose best work is never understated.

Instead, Mike Heid is a funny (some would say "crazy"), smart man who knows how to get your attention. For the past several years, he's been a writer at Peter A. Mayer Advertising in New Orleans, working on Luzianne Iced Tea, the National World War II Museum, The Roosevelt New Orleans hotel and the New Orleans Saints, among others.

Heid's work has earned him an Effie Award and several ADDY Awards at the local, regional and national levels. His friends from back home in Erie, Pennsylvania, would have to agree that he's done quite well for himself in the Deep South. (But he'll always cheer for Penn State.)

Process

"As you can see from my drawing, much of my creative process comes down to fear (a.k.a. doubt, a.k.a. insecurity). The fear hits when I'm done procrastinating, the reality of an impending deadline is setting in and I'm staring at a blank page. But

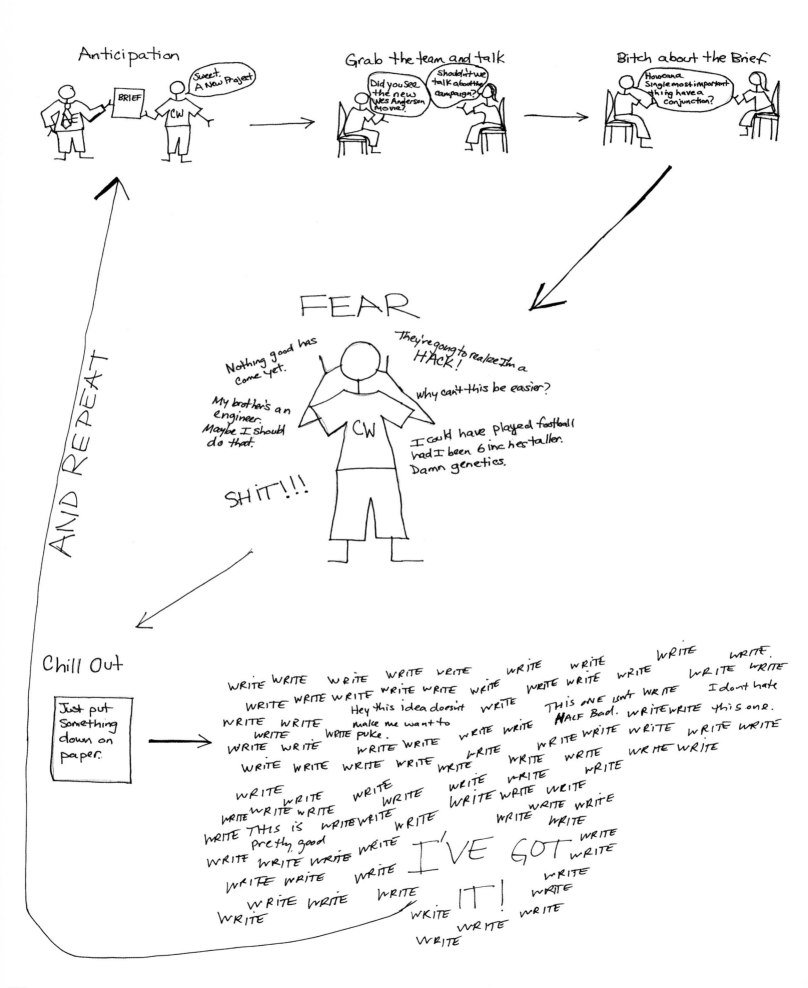

Eventually a good idea will come if I keep working at it. Sometimes that work takes a couple of hours. Sometimes it's a couple of days. Sometimes it's a couple of weeks. But in the end, the result is the same—a good idea.

fear isn't such a bad thing. You can use it to make your work even better. If you know how to deal with your fear, you can use it to push yourself to find a better idea.

"Moving past fear requires trusting your own personal process. I know that, no matter what I put down on paper—no matter how crappy that first idea may be. Eventually a good idea will come if I keep working at it. Sometimes that work takes a couple of hours. Sometimes it's a couple of days. Sometimes it's a couple of weeks. But in the end, the result is the same—a good idea. I'm not saying that I find genius every time (or ever), but 95 percent of the time, my partner and I will come up with an idea I feel good about.

"The only way you can let fear win is by not trusting your process; not believing in yourself and your ability to come up with a good idea. Believing that the fear is right—that you've already had your last good idea—that's when you've lost."

—Mike Heid

Partner

"I guess all creatives can relate to the vicious cycle in Mike's drawing. But if you're going to be caught in that cycle, you may as well roll with it.

"Though I may know him well enough to know his fear exists, Mike does a pretty good job at disguising it. His number one veil would have to be humor, including anything that involves singing, voices or dance moves of an awkward or ridiculous nature. But more importantly, his positive attitude and passion for advertising are always evident from the start of the process. He is always thinking about what different media we could

consider or what more creative approach could be taken. He seems to spend a good amount of time researching and familiarizing himself with relevant information. My guess is that this is one part procrastination, one part due diligence and one part just looking for that interesting nugget to get the conversation going.

"We take turns throwing out all the crazy, lame, irrelevant, awesome and/or unrealistic ideas. We both run them through filters and either of us can shoot them down. Ultimately, a few survive, and the pressure is off when we have something solid. But Mike will still try to one-up his best idea and come up with one more 'I got it,' even in the final stages of layout.

"Throughout the process, Mike always has a calm, collected way of challenging the strategy and selling his ideas, gracefully accepting and dishing out criticism, and if all else fails, making a fool of himself in the spirit of comic relief."

—Jill Norman, Senior Art Director, Peter A. Mayer Advertising, New Orleans

INSIGHTS FROM THE PROCESS CANVAS

All creatives experience fear. Fear is volatile because it can motivate or paralyze. You decide how to handle it, channel it and live with it.

For writers, constant rewriting and revision is part of the process. It's also a viable strategy for dealing with fear and uncertainty: from quantity comes quality.

» **"GRANDFATHER'S MUSIC" POSTER**

Agency: Peter A. Mayer Advertising, New
Orleans **Creative Director:** Josh Mayer
Art Director: Jill Norman **Writer:** Mike Heid
Client: Louisiana Philharmonic Orchestra

≽ **"MIDWAY" BILLBOARD**

Agency: Peter A. Mayer Advertising, New
Orleans **Creative Director:** Josh Mayer **Art
Director:** Missy Battle Avery **Writer:** Mike
Heid **Client:** The National World War II Museum

DAVID HORRIDGE

FOUNDER/CREATIVE DIRECTOR, THIRTY-ONE CREATIVE (AUSTIN, TEXAS)

Creative Pitch Consultant. Interim Director of Marketing. Creative Director. Writer. Art Director. Designer. Naming Consultant. Keeper of the Brand and Human Experience. That's the long and eclectic list of titles held by David Horridge over the course of his career (so far). He started as an art director at McCann Erickson in New York and a couple of years later moved to T3 in Austin, Texas, the city where he put down roots and still works today.

Horridge has worked with a broad array of clients, including Dell, Coca-Cola, Mazda, Toys"R"Us, Motorola, AT&T, Nabisco, Toshiba and Black & Decker. He's won a pile of ADDY Awards and had his work recognized by The One Show and *Print* magazine. In 1997, he founded Thirty-One Creative, a successful freelance shop offering clients a wide range of creative development experience coupled with a deep understanding of strategy. He's also actively involved in the Austin creative community, serving as education director on the board of the local American Institute of Graphic Arts (AIGA) chapter.

And there's yet another title to David Horridge's credit: professor. He taught intermediate and advanced portfolio classes for six years at the University of Texas at Austin, his alma mater.

Process

"My creative process is an act of subtractive creativity.

"First, before I uncap my Sharpie, I make sure I'm fully informed. I wallow around in every scrap of information I can find. If it's related to the problem I'm being asked to solve, I dive into it.

"Once fully submerged, the subtraction begins.

"Over the years, I've learned that the blank page is only intimidating when I feel pressured to 'add' something to it. So I don't.

Ultimately, I'm left with polished ideas. But it's the calluses that make me most proud.

I don't view the blank page as an empty canvas nor feel the artist's tug to fill it. To me, the blank page is merely a shovel and my ideas are buried deep inside my mind, usually trapped under tons of rubble.

"Much like an archaeologist who expects nothing of the first several thousand shovelfuls of dirt, I expect nothing of my ideas as I excavate my head. I dig and create piles of dirt. Nothing else.

"I also try not to critique my ideas as I unearth them. That would slow me down. I'm better when I come back and sift through everything after I get a little distance.

"When I return to my piles, I return alone. My discovery process is more of a listening one than a thinking one. I pore over everything I've dredged up. One by one, I sense the potential of each nugget, each pot shard of an idea. Does it have promise? Is it garbage? Where did I find it? Are there more? I isolate myself and I listen.

"The answers come and serve as compass points. They mark where the rich veins lie. Where I'll dig further. And so my process continues. Dig, sift, listen, repeat.

"Ultimately, I'm left with polished ideas. But it's the calluses that make me most proud."

—David Horridge

Partner

"Dave's creative process begins on the 'human' level. Although he always gains a comprehensive understanding of the product or service being offered, he quickly shifts his focus to the person he is trying to reach and attempts to relate to them on a deeper level. Who are they? What do they like to do? What makes them laugh, or cry? These questions are not answered through methodical demographic analysis, but rather through the sharing and exploration of Dave's own life experiences. Dave is very good at creating fun, organic ideation sessions that more closely resemble two friends chatting over coffee than ad creatives hard at work. His stories, humor and ideas, which might seem somewhat tangential to the exercise, frequently lead to identifying the key connections between what we are selling and the person who needs or wants it.

"For many, that might be the end of the creative exercise; find a compelling connection, write some headlines and move on. Not for Dave. The next step in his creative process is to deeply examine as many different ways to reflect those connections in the final work. He explores potential executions from every angle until one emerges that is undeniably 'right.' It's not surprising that these ideas consistently resonate with clients, consumers and award show judges alike.

"I feel lucky to have worked with someone whose creative process was as unique as it was effective. I learned a lot from Dave."

—Jonathan Balser, Chief Executive Officer,
Mooch, LLC, Atlanta

INSIGHTS FROM THE PROCESS CANVAS

Working as a freelancer affords a different perspective, a different lifestyle compared to a full-time agency role. Freelancers can set up shop wherever feels right.

For many, solitary work is essential for focus and exploration. Some prefer absolute silence while others drown out distractions with their iPod.

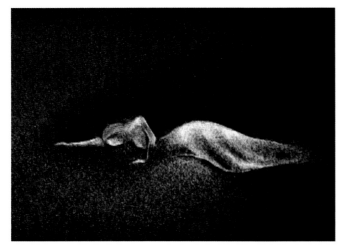 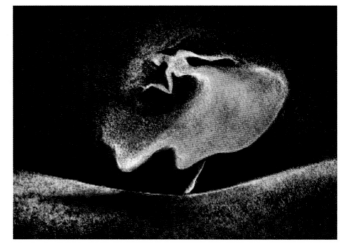

⌃ "DANCER" TV SPOT

Agency: T3, Austin, Texas **Creative Director:**
Mike Bevil **Art Director:** David Horridge **Writer:**
Jonathan Balser **Client:** Austin Lyric Opera

RACHEL HOWALD

SENIOR VICE PRESIDENT/GROUP CREATIVE DIRECTOR, McCANN ERICKSON (NEW YORK, NEW YORK)

McCANN ERICKSON

● ● ● ● ● ● ● ●

The string of awards and accolades started early in her career: Rachel Howald was named to Crain's Forty Under Forty at twenty-five, the youngest person ever to nab that honor. Since then, she's won just about every creative award in the profession, including having two of her commercials named as part of the Museum of Modern Art's permanent collection. She's also a lapsed member of Mensa,

was nominated for an Emmy in 2002, was profiled in *O, The Oprah Magazine*, and has even worked with the likes of David Crosby, who crafted some sweet music for an AT&T campaign she worked on. But, quite possibly, the accolade that rings highest on her hit parade is the one she's heard from agency colleagues and client presidents to the custodial staff in her office: Rachel Howald is so real. Funny, strategic, and a helluva writer and creative director, Howald consistently shows how good advertising can be entertaining and memorable while it makes clients like Computer Associates, Nokia, Genworth Financial, AT&T and General Mills take notice. And all the while, she remains a happy camper and fun to be around. Howald and her partner, Jennifer, are the proud moms to two sons, Cal and Will, which qualifies her for a turn in the carpool and soccer mom status in her spare time.

EAT
DO
TRY — READ — TALK
BUY   TALK — READ — THINK — TALK — TRY —
USE   DO
                                                              USE

WRITE THROW AWAY
WRITE THROW AWAY
WRITE THROW AWAY
WRITE THROW AWAY
WRITE — WRITE — THROW AWAY —
WRITE THROW AWAY
WRITE THROW AWAY
WRITE THROW AWAY

WRITE
WRITE
WRITE — THROW AWAY — IGNORE — DELAY — WRITE — READ — WRITE —
WRITE
VALUE
MOAN

DELAY
DELAY
DELAY
DELAY
DELAY
DELAY
DELAY
DELAY
DELAY
DELAY DELAY WRITE
DELAY DELAY WRITE
DELAY DELAY WRITE
DELAY WRITE WRITE
DELAY WRITE WRITE
DELAY WRITE WRITE
WRITE WRITE
WRITE WRITE WRITE
WRITE WRITE WRITE WRITE
WRITE WRITE WRITE WRITE
WRITE WRITE WRITE WRITE
WRITE WRITE WRITE WRITE
WRITE WRITE WRITE WRITE
WRITE WRITE WRITE
WRITE WRITE WRITE
WRITE WRITE
WRITE
WRITE
WRITE
WRITE
WRITE
WRITE
WRITE
WRITE
WRITE
WRITE
WRITE
WRITE
WRITE
WRITE
WRITE

☺

Well, inspiration comes from external stimuli which, when varied and rich, engages certain areas of the brain to fire synapses that correlate to electrical impulses and… I have no idea.

Process

"You know when someone asks you to explain something that you have no idea how it works but you know a little bit of terminology so you dance your way around the answer with vagaries until they eventually get tired of asking and go away? Well, inspiration comes from external stimuli which, when varied and rich, engages certain areas of the brain to fire synapses that correlate to electrical impulses and… I have no idea. I try to go to interesting places, read interesting things and talk to interesting people. Then somebody hands me a piece of paper and a deadline and I procrastinate until I eventually light candles and listen to the soundtrack to *Titanic* over and over again while I type without thinking. *Et voilà*… advertising!"

—Rachel Howald

Partner

"After twelve years of working together, here's what I can tell you about Rachel when she's working. She listens to music. Lots of it. Usually loudly. Sometimes it's Cher. Sometimes it's Klezmer. Sometimes it's jazz. And always lots of show tunes and Streisand. Oy vey, the Streisand.

"She takes notes constantly and sticks things up on the wall. She gets a giant stack of empty 4" x 6" note cards and a Sharpie and a roll of tape and goes to town, writing and sticking things up.

"When she's frustrated and we have a tight deadline, she suddenly becomes obsessed with moving around all the furniture in her office. She will spend two hours literally rearranging everything at midnight when we're supposed to be doing the final push before a big presentation. She'll move the couch, she'll clean out her desk, she'll make new playlists in her iTunes so she has a mix to move the couch to.

"On the average workday, she has a line of Starbucks cups and seltzer bottles on her desk that she works her way through as the day goes by. This leads to her other source of creative inspiration—frequent walks back and forth to the bathroom.

"Somehow it works for us. When we started our own company, she gave me a card with a Camus quote that said, 'Don't walk in front of me; I may not follow. Don't walk behind me; I may not lead. Just walk beside me and be my friend.' That's why we work together well. Neither one of us leads or follows. We just keep walking."

—Ahmer Kalam, Senior Vice President/
Group Creative Director, McCann Erickson

INSIGHTS FROM THE PROCESS CANVAS

A writer uses preparation as an important tool; many things have to happen before she's actually ready to write.

It is notable that terrific energy is involved in some of the despondency. It's dark before the dawn of a new idea.

The smile at the end, the simple understanding that the entirety of the process is worthwhile, is a confident statement and the mark of a seasoned professional.

Keep your leftovers alive.

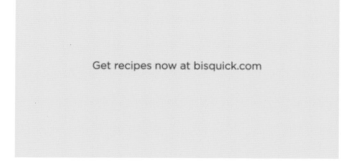

Get recipes now at bisquick.com

Bisquick

⌃ "KEEP YOUR LEFTOVERS ALIVE" TV SPOT

Agency: McCann Erickson, New York **Chief
Creative Officer:** Joyce King Thomas **Group
Creative Director/Writer:** Rachel Howald **Group
Creative Director/Art Director:** Ahmer Kalam
Agency Producer: Minnie Tran **Director:** Rocky
Morton **Client:** Bisquick, General Mills, Inc.

DAVID T. JONES

CHIEF CREATIVE OFFICER, THIRD STREET; CARTOONIST, *ADWEEK* (CHICAGO, ILLINOIS)

David T. Jones (standing) reacting to ideas.

A cartoonist's life is full of inspiration. A cartoonist/ conceptual artist/art director uses every piece of the day to get closer to the truth. David T. Jones—creator of *Adweek*'s *Ad Land* and creative director at Third Street in Chicago—must be keeping notes in a couple of big journals just to keep up.

As creative director, then executive creative director of emerging platforms at Foote, Cone & Belding in Chicago for fifteen years, Jones took on all media and a long list of brands, including Gatorade, Kraft Foods, Coors, SC Johnson, and Boeing. With that, of course, came the awards—D&AD, ADDYs, Effies, and Art Directors Club honors—plus a Webby Award in 2007. His work even landed him in *Contagious Magazine*. Now at Third Street—the Attention Agency, as they refer to themselves—he and co-founder Sean Smith deliver work that, well, grabs attention.

In fact, you've seen Jones's work and admired it. But then you've also seen some of his work and copied it, sent it to your friends with a little Post-it attached with some clever comment. You've lived his work. For a handful of years, Jones's *Ad Land* cartoon has run each week in *Adweek*. As Jones notes: "*Ad Land* has mocked, lamented, spoofed, inspired, sold out and gone viral, making fun of just about everything in advertising, nothing more than its creator."

By day, a guy doing advertising. By night, a guy dinging advertising. He does both well. Sean Smith likens it to an athlete in training. "His training—the cartoons, the humor—results in his unique ability to meet any creative opportunity," Smith says. "You never know what play is coming next, and no two are alike. Yet he's prepared for anything. That's David in the creative realm." There's probably a great cartoon idea in that statement.

When asked to describe my "CREATIVE PROCESS" the first thing I realized is that I don't really HAVE ONE.

God, I WISH it was more of a process. That sounds orderly. That sounds controlled. But, for ME at least, it's always a rough, odd journey from assignment to idea.

It all starts with the BLANK PAGE →

THIS is the single most TERRIFYING and EXCITING thing ever invented.

The NASTY thing that usually comes along for the ride is SELF DOUBT.

I suck. I suck. I suck. What if there are more new media outlets than I have ideas? I suck.

During these moments, you might even be tempted to STEAL an idea.

SO, you seek out INSPIRATION

If you don't have this reaction, you're in the wrong business.

It comes in many forms,

Save this account or you're FIRED!

but FEAR seems to be the most popular.

Steal from yourself → You might suck
Steal from award book → You probably suck.
Steal from a peer → You definitely suck.

I found this idea in one of my old sketchbooks, but can't remember if I stole it in the first place!

But the TRUTH is that IDEAS DON'T COME TO ME. The cheeky little bastards always make me come to them.

But then creatives usually get that MOJO back remembering they're hired to THEORETICALLY do the one thing nobody else can... CREATE.

Sometimes they're hiding under the stairs...

This realization often leads to that smart-ass, cynical swagger so common with creatives.

This project can't be done Half-Assed!

Dude... No worries. I'll make sure it's FULLY ASSED.

Occasionally they are on a short vacation in WISCONSIN...

Hey dere Beer!

Hey dere, Cheese!

Often they're hanging out at the neighbors...

4B

BUT...

I've found that they're rarely where you look. To paraphrase John Lennon, "Ideas are what happen when you're busy thinking of other things."

THEN somehow, thankfully, it happens. Your brain fires something juicy off in the general direction of the brief on your desk.

aahhh!

Of course, NOW you have to SELL IT!! →

The truth is that ideas don't come to me.
The cheeky little bastards always make me come to them.

Process

"The truth is that ideas don't come to me. The cheeky little bastards always make me come to them. Sometimes they're hiding under the stairs. Occasionally, they're on a short vacation to Wisconsin. Often they're hanging out at the neighbors'. But... I've found they're rarely where I look. To paraphrase John Lennon: 'Ideas are what happen when you're busy thinking other things.'"

—David T. Jones

Partner

"The focus of our business is focus. In other words, trying to get our clients to be single-minded in their communication. As I look back at all of the people I've worked with who talk about focus, David is one of the few who practices it. Probably because David epitomizes focus. And it comes across in the form of 'making you feel good about yourself.' That is the single quality that I will always remember about David. No one who meets with him comes out of that meeting feeling bad about themselves or their work. He always finds something good to say about the worst situation. It's a rare and elusive quality in a creative director. He has it, and that makes him special."

—Jonathan Harries, Vice Chairman
and Global Chief Creative Officer,
Draftfcb, Chicago

INSIGHTS FROM THE PROCESS CANVAS

"I don't have a process" feels like a contradiction when a creator takes the time to reflect on his habits.

Self-doubt happens to the most successful of idea people. The fear of hackdom seems to become more potent with every year of experience accumulated.

It can be tough enough to generate the idea. But it never really lives until the client buys it.

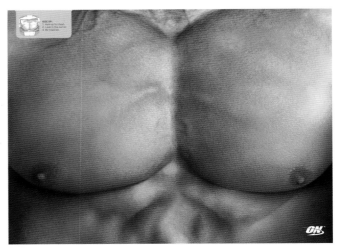

BIG LOOKS
GOOD ON YOU

GOALS MUST BE VISUALIZED.
NOW LET'S TURN THOSE GOALS INTO GAINS.

THE BIGGER PICTURE
WWW.OPTIMUMNUTRITION.COM

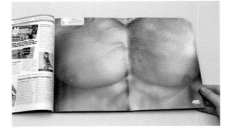

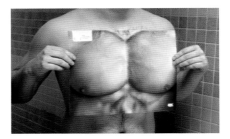

⌃ "GATEFOLD CHEST" MAGAZINE INSERT

Agency: Third Street, Chicago **Group**
Creative Director: David T. Jones **Art Director:**
Jim Haas **Writer:** David Littlejohn **Client:**
Optimum Nutrition

DAVID KENNEDY

CO-FOUNDER/CREATIVE DIRECTOR, WIEDEN+KENNEDY (PORTLAND, OREGON)

Wieden +
Kennedy

In the advertising business, Wieden+Kennedy is often referred to as W+K. But from time to time, agency co-founder David Kennedy likes to wear his own custom silk-screened, black T-shirt that reads "K+W."

Founded in 1982, Wieden+Kennedy now has offices in Portland, New York, London, Amsterdam, Shanghai, Tokyo and New Delhi. Their client list includes Nike, Coca-Cola, Miller Brewing Company, Nokia, Starbucks, Honda, ESPN, Ivory, Old Spice and Target. But no matter how big and how successful the agency becomes, at its core is the inspiration and example of the wise, funny, irreverent and fundamentally kind David Kennedy.

David is one of the most famous and honored ad men in history. He is a hall of fame laureate at both the Art Directors Club of New York and The One Club for Art & Copy. He's won Gold, Silver and Bronze Lions at the Cannes Film Festival, and his work is in the permanent collection of the Museum of Modern Art.

For the past fifteen years, David has supervised work for W+K's primary pro bono account, the American Indian College Fund (AICF). The agency has created and placed many millions of dollars worth of public service print and television ads for the thirty-seven tribal colleges supported by AICF.

The Creative Process.

(WITH APOLOGIES TO RUBE GOLDBERG)

ART DIRECTOR (A) OFFERS BANANA (B) TO MONKEY (C) MONKEY DROPS PEEL (D) WHICH CAUSES CANDLE (E) TO TO RISE, BURNING STRING (F) FLAME STARTLES SLEEPING TOMCAT (G) WHO COLLIDES WITH SPRINKLING CAN (H) WHICH EXTINGUISHES CANDLE. SEVERED STRING (F) RELEASES MALLET (I) WHICH HITS HEAD OF COPY WRITER (J), WHO, IN SEMI-CONSCIOUS STATE, PENS 3-WORD SLOGAN OF THE CENTURY. (K).

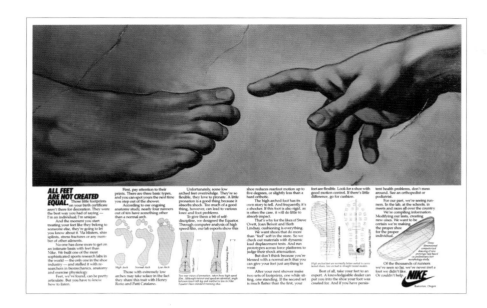

« "ALL FEET" MAGAZINE AD

Agency: Wieden+Kennedy, Portland, Oregon
Art Director: David Kennedy **Writer:** Dan
Wieden **Illustrator:** Daniel Maffia **Client:** Nike

Process

"I did not have a formal education in design, graphics or advertising. I was a fine art student—metal sculpture and printmaking—very physical stuff. Design sort of bubbled to the surface for me. I began in this business as an unschooled, inexperienced apprentice/messenger boy. I was hired only because I could draw. But I learned through osmosis.

"I always was, and continue to be, influenced by my heroes. Probably the biggest design influence on me was Push Pin Studios: Milton Glaser, Seymour Chwast and Paul Davis. I will forever be in awe of their work. They changed the world of illustration at the same time Bill Bernbach was changing the world of advertising. These are the people that seduced me into this business. To paraphrase Helmut Krone, all of these men helped elevate advertising to an art, and our jobs to a profession.

"Once I had the responsibility of tending a Lakota Sundance fire (a sacred Native American ceremony) for four nights. It occurred to me that being a creative director is similar. You have to feed the team with information, background and enthusiasm. You have to fan the flames with encouragement, fear, indifference… whatever works. But you have to let them ruminate and discover their own solutions.

"A good creative partnership is much like a marriage. Wieden+Kennedy's early success was largely due to the fact that Wieden and I were strong family men (Dan has four kids and I have five). We understand that people have to depend on and respect each other to live together successfully, whether in a home or at an office. Leo Burnett once said to me, 'You know, David, my inventory goes down the elevator every day at five o'clock.' I have never forgotten those words. At Wieden+Kennedy, our secret has been to hire people better than we are and to get the hell out of their way. We wanted to create a place where people could simply realize their potential.

"The one constant in my creative process is the hope, the prayer, the chance that I will feel the crack of the bat once more and watch the hide fly off the fucking ball as it heads for the right-field fence.

"However, if any of my own children had wanted to follow in my footsteps and become an advertising art director, I would have broken their thumbs."

—**David Kennedy**

Partner

"David Kennedy stood there in my office doorway wearing a three-piece pin-striped suit. It was the first time I ever laid eyes on him and the last time I ever saw him in that suit. After we started working together, he must've burned it or given it to Goodwill, because for the rest of his working life, with only two or three minor exceptions, this man wore Levi's and a blue work shirt. Period.

"'It simplifies things,' he said.

"Simplifying the man is a bit more difficult. There are so many facets to Kennedy, arranged in no particular order, that you cannot get a complete picture of him even after twenty-five years' exposure.

"He is completely centered, yet a mass of contradictions. In that rat's nest he called an office, the space was filled with old photos, flags, buffalo skulls, woodblock letters and other artifacts.

"We were walking back from lunch one day, trying desperately to find our way out of a business crisis. I was doing my damnedest to articulate an issue, break it down. Along the way, Kennedy listened, challenged, took another line of attack and then abruptly yelled, 'Jesus, Wieden, look!'

"There, under a tree growing out of the sidewalk, was a scrap of paper with an image I couldn't quite make out. He bent over, picked it up, brushed off the grime and flattened it out.

"'Isn't that beautiful?' He gave his classic half-laugh and looked at me with a raised eyebrow, bringing me back to the present moment and that piece of flotsam back to the office.

"He is addicted to beauty. He can't leave it alone. It is this obsession with craftsmanship—coupled with his startling conceptual talent—that has guided Wieden+Kennedy from the backwoods of Oregon out onto the international stage.

"I owe him everything.

"His Indian name is Wichasha Owayakepi Chunta, which is Lakota for He Who Sees the World With His Heart.

"He has contributed so much to this industry, so much to our agency. But of all the things he has given me, and they are many, the most enduring are those three simple words:

"'Jesus, Wieden, look.'"

—Dan Wieden, Co-Founder/Creative
Director, Wieden+Kennedy

INSIGHTS FROM THE PROCESS CANVAS

Even the most accomplished creative people have heroes, others whose work inspires and pushes them to be better.

The creative process is both highly serendipitous and fraught with the potential for mistakes and even failure. Understanding this and learning from it is key.

≫ "THINK INDIAN" TV SPOT

Agency: Wieden+Kennedy, Portland, Oregon
Creative Directors: Dan Wieden, David Kennedy
Executive Creative Directors: Mark Fitzloff,
Susan Hoffman **Art Director:** Patty Fogarty
Writers: Justin "Scrappers" Morrison, Patty
Fogarty **Client:** American Indian College Fund

≫ "ON THE REZ" MAGAZINE AD

Tagline: Educating the mind and spirit. **Agency:**
Wieden+Kennedy, Portland, Oregon **Executive
Creative Director:** Dan Wieden **Creative Director:**
David Kennedy **Art Director:** Patty Fogarty
Writer: Will Ulbricht **Client:** American Indian
College Fund

JANET KESTIN/ NANCY VONK

CO-CHIEF CREATIVE OFFICERS, OGILVY & MATHER (TORONTO, CANADA)

© 2009 Farokh Monajem

What happens when two women in advertising challenge everything that's wrong with advertising that targets women? Ask Janet Kestin and Nancy Vonk. In 2007, they took the beauty industry to task and promoted the power of self-esteem in the "Campaign for Real Beauty" for Dove. *Newsweek*, *Time* and the *Wall Street Journal* took notice, all listing their work among the top ten ads of the year. Now that's how to sell some soap.

Kestin and Vonk, two of the most powerful and accomplished women in advertising, started working together in 1991. Since then, they've won Cannes Grand Prix awards, One Show Pencils, Clios—just about every honor in the industry. *Creativity* magazine ranked them among the Top 50 Creative People in 2008, and in 2007 they were named advertising's women of the year by both the Women's Image Network (WIN) in Los Angeles and the Advertising Women of New York (AWNY).

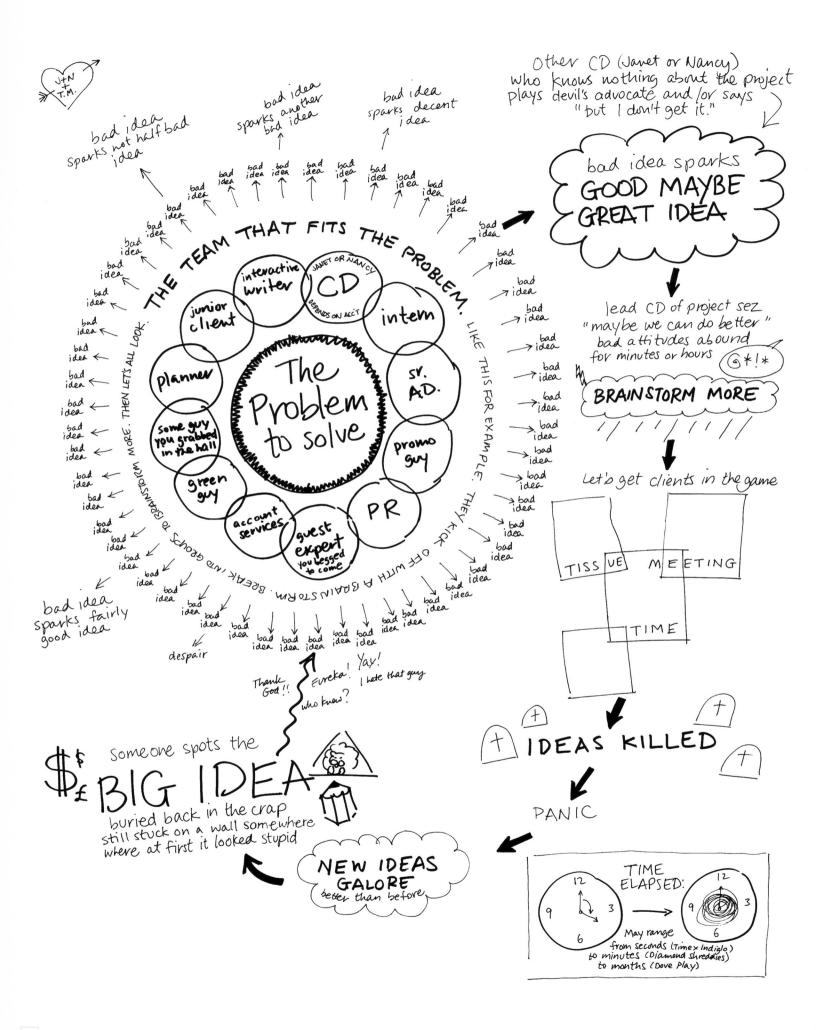

They've been busy. But never too busy to mentor young people and help them find a place in the business. For years now, Kestin and Vonk have written the popular advice column, "Ask Jancy" on the website IHAVEANIDEA (ihaveanidea. org). They also wrote a book, *Pick Me*, in 2005, sharing their insights about building portfolios and job hunting.

They are role models for women entering this business. But all you guys should be taking notes, too.

Process

"Quantity leads to quality. This observation had a huge impact on Janet and me. Generate a huge pile of (mostly) crappy ideas, as fast as possible. This makes it impossible for your brain to edit or pass judgment (that unfortunate, built-in idea-killer we all have in our hard drives). The law of averages means in a pile of one hundred ideas, spit out in minutes, there will be at least one thought-starter that will get you somewhere. And often, reviewing the pile, some god-awful ideas can trigger great ideas. Nothing is more terrifying than the blank page, at the beginning of any project. Now we leapfrog past the paralysis stage.

"The other fundamental difference in the way I look at getting to big ideas is a media-neutral starting point. The lens you put on chasing a good television spot, for instance, ('so I'll need a tight little story that works well in thirty seconds') is entirely different from thinking, 'What will solve the problem?' Hunting

⌃ "EVOLUTION" TV SPOT

Agency: Ogilvy & Mather, Toronto, Canada
Chief Creative Officers: Janet Kestin, Nancy Vonk **Art Directors:** Tim Piper, Mike Kirkland
Writer: Tim Piper **Client:** Dove, Unilever Canada

Unilever Canada, a division of Unilever Canada, Inc.

for a solution to the fundamental business problem leads to a big idea that can then inform many media.

"Another big leg up on the search for great ideas is perspective from many corners. Getting brain cells from not only the core team but also outsiders with experience in other disciplines (and industries, when possible), plus brand-new, non-jaded brains packed with creativity (right out of school) is ideal. I try to get the team together at the outset, as soon as I know the business challenge/opportunity—even before there's a formal briefing document. There never seems to be enough time on a work-back schedule for creative development. Even if the strategy or conditions change in the meantime, this is rarely wasted energy."

—Nancy Vonk

Partner

"I love Janet's partnership in looking for answers. Environment is always important, and her house is ideal: have a tea, have this home made something I just made, get comfortable on my vintage couch. Let's get some breeze going and start gabbing. Get the gossip out of the way. Then: Charge. (We encourage people to work where they think best. Often that's outside an office full of distractions.)

"Janet is non-judgmental, staring at ideas. She's so good at the delicate back and forth—if she doesn't like something, it doesn't feel like a moment of failure, just a chance to keep going and get to something smarter, more fun, better. She's relentlessly truthful, encouraging, kind. Unlike me, Miss

Cut-to-the-Chase. We are yin-yang on the hunt. We often start with Tom Monahan's 100 mph thinking exercise. From there, I count on Janet's creativity, intuition and intelligence to help get to something really interesting. Watching, you'd see talking talking talking silence while we scribble, then more talking, more scribbling, energy levels ranging over the hours from wound up to catatonic. And although she's the copywriter, me the art director, her pad is full of images, mine with words. I can trust her with my fragile ego, bad ideas and potential solutions. The best moment in this business is the one where you recognize a big idea. It might have popped out right at the start, or weeks into the search. I'll always remember Janet blurting out the big idea for one of our best campaigns right at the client briefing. There's no one I'd rather be in the trenches with to figure out the puzzle."

—Nancy Vonk

INSIGHTS FROM THE PROCESS CANVAS

From one of the most famous teams in the business, a tribute to teamwork.

Never discount the bad ideas. Sometimes good ones are hiding inside them.

A moment of silence, please, for the ideas that get killed. They are casualties of every project.

⌃ ›› "DIAMOND SHREDDIES" OUTDOOR AND PACKAGE REDESIGN

Agency: Ogilvy & Mather, Toronto, Canada **Chief Creative Officers:** Janet Kestin, Nancy Vonk **Art Director:** Ivan Pols **Writers:** Hunter Somerville, Tim Piper **Client:** Shreddies, Post Cereals

MIKE LESCARBEAU

CHIEF EXECUTIVE OFFICER, CARMICHAEL LYNCH (MINNEAPOLIS, MINNESOTA)

Carmichael Lynch

Mike Lescarbeau is known as the guy who can revamp complex organizational systems, write copy that breathes life into brands, and still offer a lopsided grin as part of his executive duties. Few others in the business multitask so well from the executive suite.

Lescarbeau was an early advocate of campaigns that employ new media. In 2001, he launched One and All in Minneapolis as a fully integrated creative resource. The agency won the 4A's O'Toole Award, which recognizes creative excellence across all media, in its first year of eligibility.

Lescarbeau joined Carmichael Lynch as president and chief creative officer from Ogilvy & Mather in New York. Prior to that, he held creative and management positions at Fallon Worldwide, Leagas Delaney and Hill Holiday, where he won Cannes Lions, Effies and One Show Pencils galore.

At Carmichael Lynch, he has reorganized workflow to include media and production insights at the conceptual stage of creative development, resulting in first-time recognition for the agency's online product from the Favourite Website Awards and *Creativity*. He is responsible for creative work on behalf of all of the agency's clients, which include Harley-Davidson, Jack Link's Beef Jerky and Subaru. In coming to the venerable Carmichael Lynch, Lescarbeau reminded the advertising

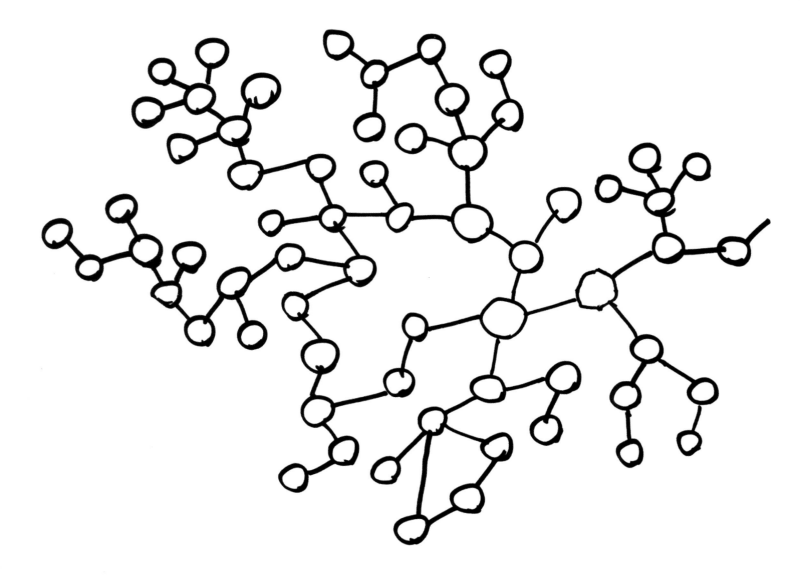

My drawing falls way short of being an accurate depiction of my creative process, mainly because procrastination is a difficult concept to visualize.

world that the Minneapolis school of advertising continues to do incredible work with one of its own leading the way.

Process

"There isn't an iPhone application for ideas, but if we ever really do map the route to great big thoughts, I'm sure iDea won't be far behind. Given the way Carmichael Lynch makes its money, then, why would I even participate in this exercise? Because I was sure it was hopeless, that's why.

"But then, as my drawing took shape, it started to remind me of something: the models used in network science, that scary new discipline that codifies what were once seen as random associations.

"My drawing falls way short of being an accurate depiction of my creative process, mainly because procrastination is a difficult concept to visualize. But assuming some of the connecting lines between thoughts (the circles) are actually me going to the movies or looking at completely off-topic websites, I guess this about sums it up. One thought leads to another, which can lead to several others, and so on, until I arrive at a useful idea.

"Or not. Sometimes the process just keeps me busy while my partner thinks of something great. I stopped mid-effort, fearful of providing a nugget to some enterprising software developer. Then I started phoning my colleagues, begging them to self-censor."

—Mike Lescarbeau

Partner

"How to work with Mike Lescarbeau:

Don't expect to sit in an office and grind out concepts. Mike is too ADD for that.

Listen carefully to his stream-of-consciousness ramblings. You may think he's just walking down the hall and talking, but he's actually concepting. Interspersed in his rambling are headlines and storylines. Keep an ear open for them.

Don't expect him to tell you how great his ideas are. Mike is too humble to hand you a single piece of paper and say,

'Here's the solution.' I've seen him deliver a brilliant idea with a scribble and a shrug.

Don't expect the expected. He will question the brief, question the media, question everything except the need to deliver the proposition to the audience in a way that makes them take notice.

Even though Mike practically invented the 'stupid factor' in copywriting humor, don't expect funny concepts if funny isn't the appropriate voice for the campaign. Some of his best work has more poignancy than humor.

Despite his 'don't gimme none of that book learnin'' persona, Mike is a well-read, worldly gentleman. So he's a quick study when it comes to relating and talking to just about any audience.

Don't tinker with his writing too much or you'll wreck it. I know, because I've done it and regretted it.

Do expect to have fun.

"Working with Mike was like playing tennis with someone better than me who has the grace not to pummel me, but patiently brings me up to their level. While some smart people use their smarts to elevate themselves, Mike uses his smarts to elevate everyone in the room."

—Tom Lichtenheld, Art Director, Artist and Author, Geneva, Illinois

INSIGHTS FROM THE PROCESS CANVAS

Associative thinking is a powerful tool that links one idea to another; this process canvas shows its possibilities.

Sometimes the slightest change of perspective offers a new set of conceptual opportunities.

A simple drawing shows us the bare bones skeleton of a great idea. What a wonderful 3-D hologram this would make.

≪ SUBARU "LOVE" TV SPOT

Agency: Carmichael Lynch, Minneapolis **Creative Directors:** Randy Hughes, Mike Lescarbeau, Jim Nelson **Director of Integrated Production:** Joe Grundhoefer **Senior Executive Integrated Producer:** Brynn Hausmann **Director:** Scott Hicks, Independent Media **Director of Photography:** Wally Pfister **Executive Producer:** Susanne Preissler **Client:** Subaru

KATE LUMMUS

WRITER, PUBLICIS MODEM (NEW YORK, NEW YORK)

The first thing you need to know about Kate Lummus is that she's from Texas. This is important for a few reasons; it explains her excessive use of "y'all" and her polite yet rebellious nature. And she's quick to explain: She's not a Katherine, Katie or Kaitlyn. Just Kate.

Having started her career in New York City, she's been lucky enough to get experience with both integrated and digital advertising and the opportunity to work on many global brands and well-known campaigns. At Atmosphere BBDO, Lummus helped establish FedEx online, with an interactive video site, simple brand banners and out-of-home installations. She also helped pitch and win the Lay's account, worked on the branding merger of Cingular and AT&T, and dabbled in the Citi business. At Publicis Modem, Lummus works on everything from packaged goods to luxury brands.

Lummus is adventurous. She worked on Capitol Hill as a junior in college, interning for Hillary Clinton. She grew up overseas, living on six continents before the age of fourteen, and loves to travel. That character and spirit shows up in her work.

Process

"I'm not entirely sure how it all comes together.

I TAKE AN IDEA APART AND THEN
PUT IT BACK TOGETHER

IT'S WHAT'S IN BETWEEN
THAT IS THE
MOST INTERESTING.

COP A FEEL

Get to know your girls.
Get regular screenings and get to know
what is normal for you. Tell your doctor if
anything changes to help catch breast cancer early.

know your girls   lower your risk   take the pledge
www.facebook.com/YoplaitPledge

« "COP A FEEL" MAGAZINE AD

Agency: Publicis Modem, New York **Executive Creative Director:** Patrick Clarke **Creative Director:** Roald van Wyk **Art Director:** Katie Kuni **Writer:** Kate Lummus **Client:** Yoplait, General Mills, Inc.

©2009 Yoplait USA, Inc.

"All I know is that I trust my brain.

"I know this may sound egotistic, but it works. If I believe I will have the idea, it will come. A sort of mind-field of dreams. Because once that failure pressure is gone, my brain is free to do its thing.

"So I fill it with all the little pieces it might need to put an idea together. I try the product, I read catalogs and blogs and online product reviews. I go to movies I wouldn't normally see, or car shows, or concerts. I just keep going over it in my head. It's all there. It just hasn't been rearranged, revised, rewritten yet.

"Briefs will try to put it together for you, analyze it and tell you what it means. But I already know the idea isn't in the brief. Because the idea is in my head. Somewhere.

"So I rip it up, rearrange it, undo it, decode it and unwind it until I'm out of material.

"Then I get the tape."

—Kate Lummus

Partner

"I have been working with Kate for almost four years. Even though we have been working together for a while, I cannot say exactly what her creative process is, since I am not inside her head.

"But from the outside, her creative process seems like this:

"While the ideas do come from her brain, they are seriously triggered by so many things around her. Not just product research, or staring at walls. I've seen her come up with ideas about a yogurt supporting breast cancer by watching an MTV show about douchebag boyfriends. They may not seem at first like they are a logical pair, but the angle at which she pieced them together formed a really great idea. She takes all these environmental factors and tries them out with the idea, piecing them all together. It's as if she looks at every idea in a 360-degree mirror all at once, combining it with every related concept. Someone may interpret the idea from one angle, and she attacks all angles. This all combines to form very unique, singular ideas."

—Katie Kuni, Art Director, Publicis Modem

INSIGHTS FROM THE PROCESS CANVAS

The youngest professional in this book ripped the process canvas to shreds. That's bold. It's a nice quality in a writer, too.

The deconstruction here, both literal and figurative, challenges the preconceived and asserts the need for developing one's own perspective on the problem.

Help stop breast cancer from being the leading cause of cancer death in young women.

Know your girls.
Lower your risk.
Take the pledge.

susan G.
komen
FOR THE cure

For every pledge we receive by October 31, 2009, Yoplait® will donate 10 cents to Susan G. Komen® for the Cure, up to $100,000.

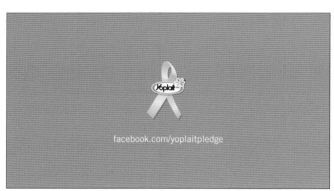

facebook.com/yoplaitpledge

≈ "KNOW YOUR GIRLS" VIRAL ONLINE AD

Agency: Publicis Modem, New York **Executive Creative Director:** Patrick Clarke **Creative Director:** Roald van Wyk **Art Director:** Katie Kuni **Writer:** Kate Lummus **Client:** Yoplait, General Mills, Inc.

©2009 Yoplait USA, Inc.

SIMON MAINWARING

CREATIVE DIRECTOR/WRITER, FREELANCE AND CONSULTANCY (LOS ANGELES, CALIFORNIA)

Saatchi & Saatchi, TBWA\Chiat\Day, Leagas Delaney, and Goodby, Silverstein & Partners, and has picked up more than eighty international awards at Cannes Lions, The One Show, and D&AD. A colleague tells us: "Simon is the guy who reminds us we really can do something of value for the world if we fight for it. He demands that we own our integrity."

Today, through his brand consultancy firm, Mainwaring is broadening his influence. His social media clients include TED Prize, ONE, Clinton Global Initiative and the X PRIZE Foundation, while his philanthropic work includes the Environmental Protection Authority in Australia, the Multiple Sclerosis Society in London, the Robin Hood Foundation's Uncommon Schools project and the American Diabetes Association. Mainwaring writes for the online sites PSFK, Brain Pickings and Social Media Today, while his own blog focuses on how the intersection between branding, technology and

Simon Mainwaring believes in staying ahead of the curve. His work over the last twenty years proves it: Besides Nike and Motorola, he's been the creative brand leader on News Corporation's Global Energy Initiative, Las Vegas's carbon-neutral "Zero City" Project, as well as the launch of all three generations of the Toyota Prius. Along the way, he's worked at Ogilvy & Mather, Wieden+Kennedy,

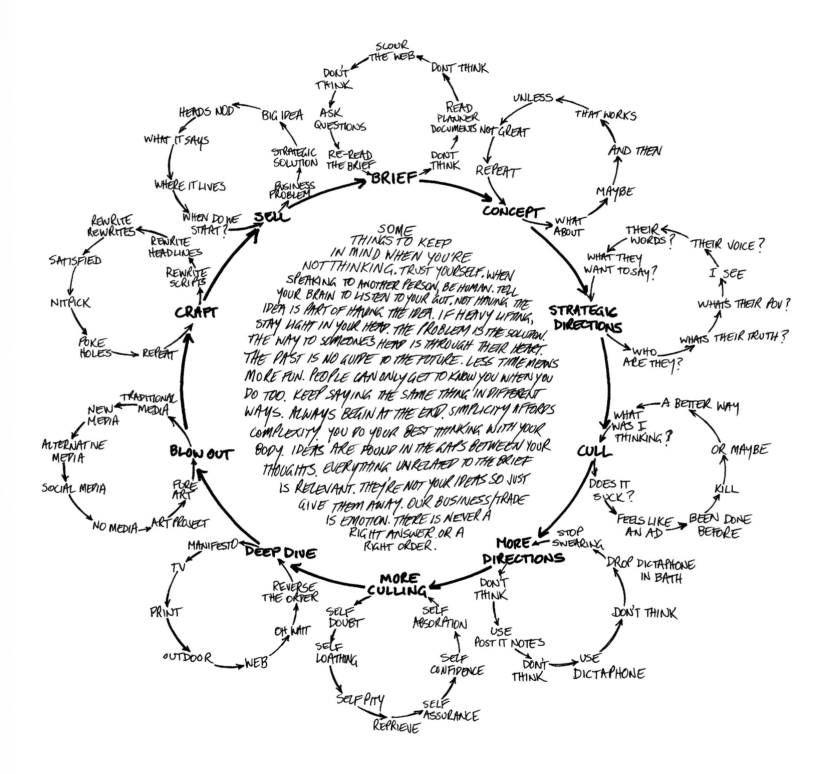

SOME THINGS TO KEEP IN MIND WHEN YOU'RE NOT THINKING. TRUST YOURSELF. WHEN SPEAKING TO ANOTHER PERSON, BE HUMAN. TELL YOUR BRAIN TO LISTEN TO YOUR GUT. NOT HAVING THE IDEA IS PART OF HAVING THE IDEA. IF HEAVY LIFTING, STAY LIGHT IN YOUR HEAD. THE PROBLEM IS THE SOLUTION. THE WAY TO SOMEONE'S HEAD IS THROUGH THEIR HEART. THE PAST IS NO GUIDE TO THE FUTURE. LESS TIME MEANS MORE FUN. PEOPLE CAN ONLY GET TO KNOW YOU WHEN YOU DO TOO. KEEP SAYING THE SAME THING IN DIFFERENT WAYS. ALWAYS BEGIN AT THE END. SIMPLICITY AFFORDS COMPLEXITY. YOU DO YOUR BEST THINKING WITH YOUR BODY. IDEAS ARE FOUND IN THE GAPS BETWEEN YOUR THOUGHTS. EVERYTHING UNRELATED TO THE BRIEF IS RELEVANT. THEY'RE NOT YOUR IDEAS SO JUST GIVE THEM AWAY. OUR BUSINESS/TRADE IS EMOTION. THERE IS NEVER A RIGHT ANSWER OR A RIGHT ORDER.

My only wish is that I would have learned earlier that I do not need to prove anything to others or myself.

social media is changing our lives. His upcoming book will forecast how social media can transform our world.

Mainwaring studied law and fine arts at the University of Sydney, theater with Larry Moss in New York and voice with Patsy Rodenburg at London's Royal National Theater. He's a dad and an Australian, and he believes you can only see what's coming if you stay out front. So, that's where you'll find him, ahead of the curve and urging us all to follow.

Process

"It took me a long time to learn that good ideas are simple, emotional and human. It's an easy thing to say, but it takes training and a lot of mistakes to get to the point where you instinctively think that way.

"That means I have a reckless but hard-won trust of my first thought, 'gut' reactions; a solid commitment not to over-think; a profound respect for the work the brain does when it's not thinking about something. And a core belief that if you want to create anything new, you must always look outside your own work or industry for inspiration.

"The moment when an idea reveals itself is as much a thrill today as it was twenty years ago. My only wish is that I would have learned earlier that I do not need to prove anything to others or myself. That pressure only gets in the way of us doing justice to our creative potential.

"No matter how we approach creative work, it should be fun. The arts are an enormous playroom where we get to behave like children, never looking for answers where we are told to, but instead heading off in unknown directions. The joy comes in the surprise of finding what we didn't know was there. There is great power in approaching life this way, leaving us free to discover the answers only creativity can find and, in so doing, revealing our shared humanity."

—Simon Mainwaring

Partner

"As I write this note in honor of Simon's 'singular' creative prowess, I am reminded that one simple, honest—perhaps even dull—idea (when one has a good partner) will always lead to the next 'slightly better' idea, which then leads to the next and so forth and so on.

"They are stories told to each other. Napkins sketched and scribbled on. They are hours and days (usually hours, given the state of advertising today) searching and then finding.

"It is my understanding and witness that Simon excels in this team dynamic. This quality, again, in my opinion, is Simon's first and best compliment, to be sure.

"It is his absolute adherence to pop culture that inspires. This is the nucleus of his idea generating.

"As we start down the creative path, he and I, we adhere to a strict 'blank-stare policy'—not knowing what, if anything, will come to mind or, worse, worrying if we are finally that one beer past our limit on creative brain cell depletion.

"And then, as we always do, we course-correct and restart the process:

"Simon: What's happening right now in culture? How can we—right now—affect positive change? Is the brand's core belief valid and living in real time? Is their brand behavior bold enough? How can we insert our client into the very center of change sweeping the cultural landscape? What do they have to offer? What conversations are taking place? How can we be a part of those conversations? Where are those conversations intersecting? Should our client follow pop culture or lead pop culture?

"Joe: Should we order lunch?

"And then, as we always do, we tell a great story."

—Joe Shands, Creative Director, TBWA\ Chiat\Day, Los Angeles

INSIGHTS FROM THE PROCESS CANVAS

Here's an impressive decision tree covering all contingencies. That's a mark of experience.

A Janusian awareness of paradox is clear: Simplicity affords complexity; everything unrelated is relevant; always begin at the end.

Culling and editing involves both self-doubt and self-confidence.

CAL McALLISTER

CO-FOUNDER/CREATIVE DIRECTOR, WEXLEY SCHOOL FOR GIRLS (SEATTLE, WASHINGTON)

© 2010 Karen Kuehn, www.karenkuehn.com

Cal McAllister is a proud Detroit native who cut his teeth as a beat writer for *Chicago Tribune*. After getting in a lot of trouble for making things up, he switched to advertising.

Before co-founding Wexley School for Girls with Ian Cohen in 2003, he worked on regional, national and international business at small shops such as WONGDOODY and global agencies such as Foote, Cone & Belding and Publicis Worldwide. He's worked on the brands Nike, ESPN, Microsoft, Xbox, T-Mobile, Mothers Against Drunk Driving (MADD), Coca-Cola, the American Red Cross, Amstel Light and NASCAR, to name a few.

His work has been recognized by almost every international advertising award show and journal, including the Cannes Lions, the Clios, *Communication Arts*, the Art Directors Club and The One Show. As a screenwriter, his films have been selected by and screened at the Seattle International Film Festival, Slamdance, the Chicago Short Film Festival, AtomFilms and the RESFEST International Film Festival, among others.

Cal's six-year-old niece, Louisa, offers this: "Uncle Cow is a man, and he is nice! He is a joyfle man. He has 2 neeses, and 1 nefuwe. He likes chikins. He has soft scruffy hair. He has a nice wife named Amanda who takes showers 100 times a day. He has a verey good tast. He is a strong man. He is a writer

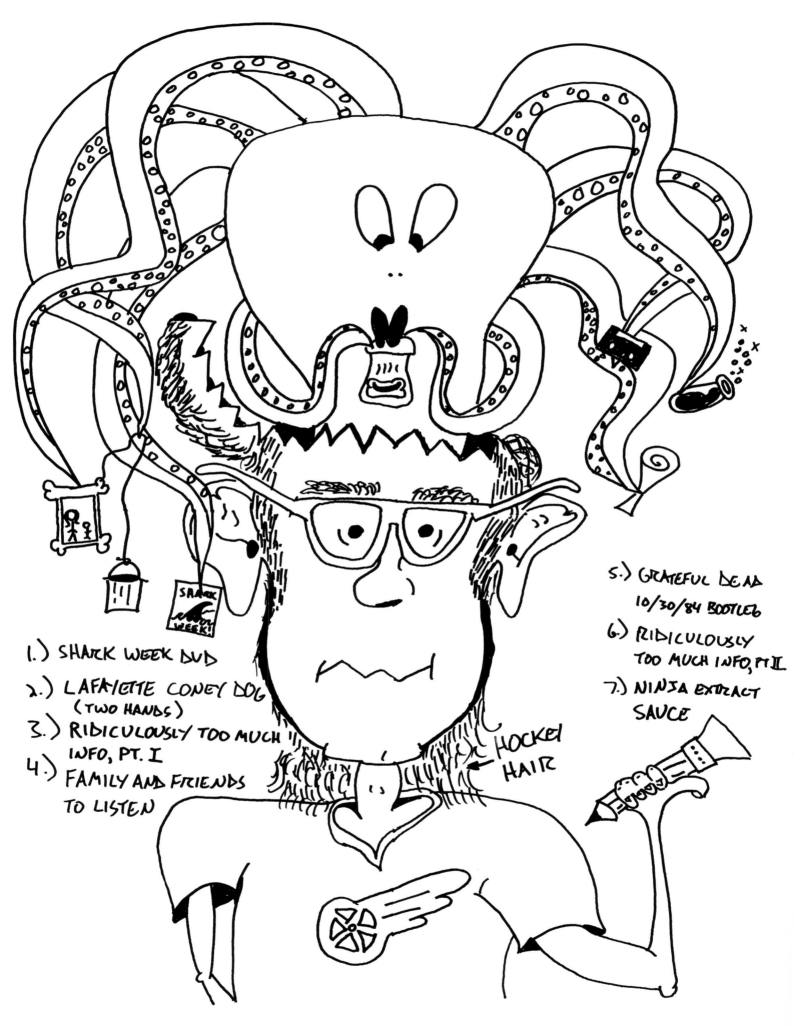

1.) SHARK WEEK DVD
2.) LAFAYETTE CONEY DOG (TWO HANDS)
3.) RIDICULOUSLY TOO MUCH INFO, PT. I
4.) FAMILY AND FRIENDS TO LISTEN
5.) GRATEFUL DEAD 10/30/84 BOOTLEG
6.) RIDICULOUSLY TOO MUCH INFO, PT II
7.) NINJA EXTRACT SAUCE

SHARK WEEK!

HOCKEY HAIR

I like to hear little stories, little truths, and see how they tie together. Then I'll make something up to keep it interesting.

at Wexley School for girls. His favorite house anamle is a dog. And he is a verey good prson."

Process

"I am happiest with too much information. Some folks feel that contaminates their thinking, gets them too close to the product. I'm the other way around. I have a journalism degree and was a *Chicago Tribune* reporter when I first graduated from Ohio State, so maybe it was the training.

"Go get lots and lots of material and sculpt and sandblast and whittle it down to relevancy. Then do it again.

"I don't consider myself a great creator. I like to hear little stories, little truths, and see how they tie together. Then I'll make something up to keep it interesting. But I need to start somewhere."

—Cal McAllister

Partner

"Cal and I think pretty similarly. We tend to approach our work in short creative bursts. It seems to me that he likes to put

just enough time pressure on himself so that the creative will explode from that pressure. He also wants enough time to edit and think through ideas. He likes the little details. He likes to fire off a lot of random ideas and approach every single problem, no matter how small, like he can create something amazing for it. So, in that sense, to use a football analogy, he rarely takes a play off."

—Ian Cohen, Co-Founder/Creative Director,
Wexley School for Girls

INSIGHTS FROM THE PROCESS CANVAS

Creative pros must know how to multitask (think: octopus). Multiple projects for multiple clients are always in play, each at different stages with their own demands for the mind's attention.

The world around us offers context. Everything we experience informs and influences creative thinking, whether or not it has anything to do with advertising.

» **"PARKING SPACE" AMBIENT AD**

Agency: Wexley School for Girls, Seattle
Art Director: Kohl Norville **Writer:** Cal McAllister **Client:** Mothers Against Drunk Driving (MADD)

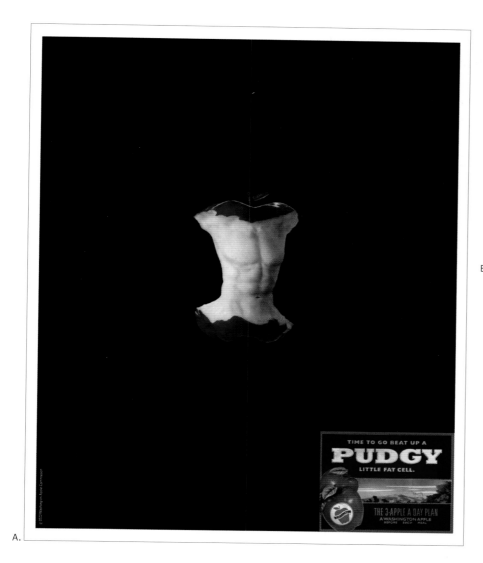

A.

B.

« ⌃ "THE 3-APPLE A DAY PLAN" MAGAZINE ADS

A. Headline: Time to go beat up a pudgy little fat cell. B. Headline: A few apples a day keeps the lipo doctor away. Agency: Wexley School for Girls, Seattle Art Director: Rob Rich Writer: Cal McAllister Client: Washington Apple Commission

JIM MOUNTJOY

FOUNDING PARTNER/EXECUTIVE VICE PRESIDENT/CREATIVE DIRECTOR,
LOEFFLER KETCHUM MOUNTJOY (CHARLOTTE, NORTH CAROLINA)

Photo by Jimmy Williams ©2009.

Jim Mountjoy (second from left) enjoying the great outdoors.

North Carolina owes a debt to Jim Mountjoy. His thirty-plus-year career has been spent in Charlotte at the agency that bears his name, Loeffler Ketchum Mountjoy, started with a couple of friends and a couple of clients before he had graduated college. He's kept talent and vision at home—even as he took national and international honors in The One Show, the Art Directors Club, *Communication Arts*, *Graphis* and other shows—and was named twice by *Adweek* as the Southeast's top creative director. He is also a three-time finalist for the MPA Kelly Award for the best magazine ad campaign in America. It's not hard to figure out why the University of North Carolina named Jim to its hall of fame.

His breathtaking work for North Carolina Travel and Tourism Division and Outward Bound show his investment in the state: LKM's tourism ads teach us all how visualizations of natural beauty can help drive an economy. His careful

creative brief

creaitve berif

cretaiev brfie

ceravtie bifre

acvieert bfrie

cretieva fribe

vrceteiafibre

retvaciebifre

tevcaeirfrieb

ebvaervcift

bvercitief

bitrvifae

tfiveart

fverita

ivetirfa

afrtiei

eartif

tferai

refiat

itefa

iefa

ifea

idea

Creative leadership is expected of you and you have the responsibility to take bolder steps that are needed to transcend rote thinking and answers.

creative mentorship of some of the country's best thinkers over the years inspires young creatives, many of them thinking, "It's either New York or Charlotte, North Carolina, for me." That's power.

Mountjoy has built a reputation as a gracious and generous teacher, mentor and industry leader. He served on the board of directors for The One Club and currently serves on the board of advisors for Creative Circus, an Atlanta portfolio school for advertising and design. He's now teaching and building creative curriculum at Queens University of Charlotte, another lasting gift to his home state.

Process

"Creativity is about building trust. First, you prove to people and yourself you are disciplined enough to cross your t's and dot your i's in all the basics as well as being responsible to others. From there, you move to a more intimate and deeper knowledge of the needs, expectations and goals of others and synthesize this into original insights that are valued. Next, it's usually at this stage others begin to not only trust you, but place a measure of faith in your ideas and actions. Now creative leadership is expected of you and you have the responsibility to take bolder steps that are needed to transcend rote thinking and answers. Sounds a bit scientific, but the art is in doing it every day with passion."

—Jim Mountjoy

Partner

"Every time I've gotten an assignment from Jim Mountjoy, it was serious. Meaning I never got the ad-world run around.

The ideas I was asked to execute were as clear as a bell on a Sunday morning in an Italian village.

"I always loved and respected his solution to a communication brief from his clients, be it tourism, flooring or handmade windows. He has a wonderful way with words, and I wished I had recorded the telephonic briefs I've gotten over the years. I was allowed to be my best at all times and never expected to second-guess what someone else may think of my interpretation of his ideas. The atmosphere that created was sublime. He would always bring something extra to the table while on a shoot, as his mind was constantly working at keeping the thought process alive: Here's another ball—run with it, dude. What a privilege.

"Not to mention his 'Southern' humor. Every shoot had a huge quota of belly laughs, day and night, be it driving through the North Carolina landscape or walking in the freezing cold in Manhattan. Jim Mountjoy is a Southern gentleman who has graced the American advertising community with his wit and brilliant thinking."

—Harry De Zitter, Photographer,
Naples, Florida

INSIGHTS FROM THE PROCESS CANVAS

Many creatives don't respect creative briefs. Here's one who does. Look at how he uses it.

Ideas evolve. Finding simplicity leads to elegance.

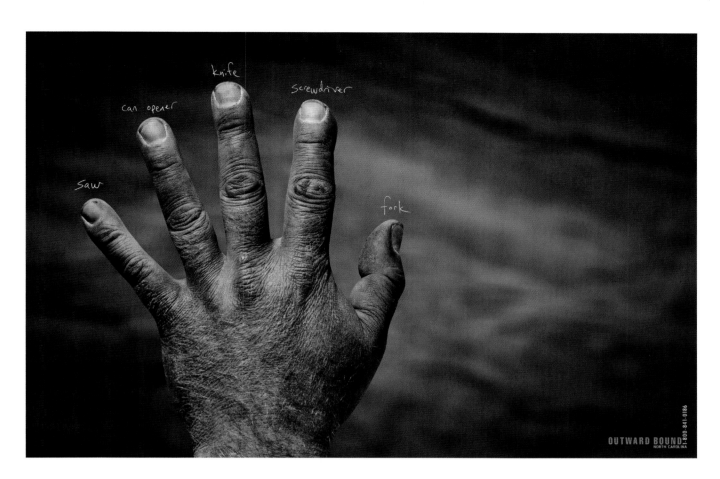

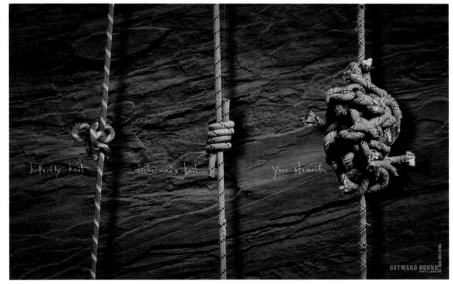

⌃ « "HAND" AND "ROPE" MAGAZINE ADS

Agency: Loeffler Ketchum Mountjoy, Charlotte, North Carolina **Creative Director:** Jim Mountjoy **Art Director:** Doug Pedersen **Writer:** Curtis Smith **Client:** Outward Bound

DOUG PEDERSEN

ASSOCIATE CREATIVE DIRECTOR/ART DIRECTOR, CARMICHAEL LYNCH (MINNEAPOLIS, MINNESOTA)

Carmichael Lynch

Sometimes it pays to be a regular guy with remarkable talent. It makes other talented people want to work with you. It builds your career. It lets you make choices about where you want to live and how you want that life to be.

Doug Pedersen is living proof of this. Courted by many agencies because of his remarkable junior book, Pedersen landed at Loeffler Ketchum Mountjoy in North Carolina, a wonderland of talented people in a small, designerly agency with mentors like Jim Mountjoy to guide him. In his first two years, he won more awards—Gold Pencils, Cannes Lions—than he might have ever dreamed.

Pedersen stayed at LKM for nine years and worked on the Outward Bound and North Carolina tourism projects to the benefit of the agency's clients and his own career. From there,

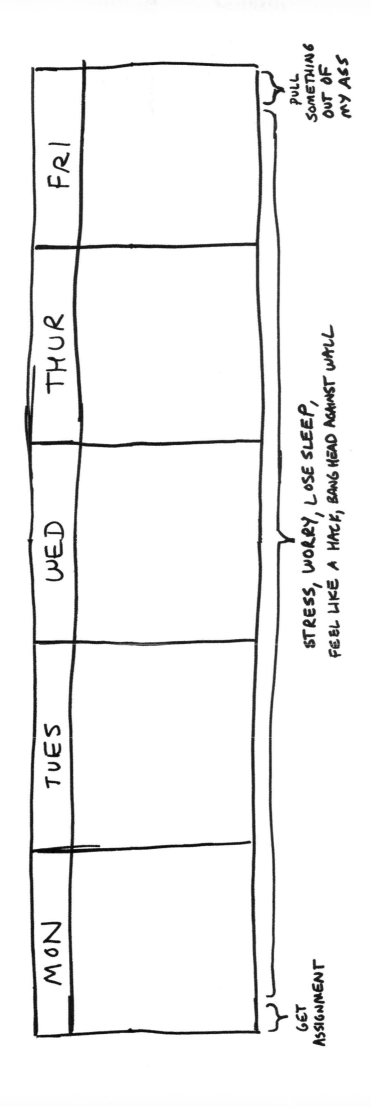

Headline: The extended forecast calls for periods of peace followed by quiet. **Agency:** Carmichael Lynch, Minneapolis **Creative Director:** Mike Haeg **Art Director:** Doug Pedersen **Creative Director/Writer:** Heath Pochucha **Client:** Bell Canoe Works

The extended forecast calls for periods of peace followed by quiet

BELL
CANOE WORKS

he headed to Crispin Porter + Bogusky in Miami, and later, Carmichael Lynch in Minneapolis.

Over the course of his career, he has helped produce advertising campaigns for Volkswagen, Harley-Davidson, Subaru, Burger King, Miller Lite and a long list of others.

Maybe the best part of the story is that he remains a grounded, good guy. "Nicest guy, I know," they say. "And with all that talent. What a package."

Process

"The Big Stuff:

"To do truly great work, you have to see your work as more than just work. You have an almost unhealthy obsession with creating great ideas and crafting them.

"But you have to have someone in your life who helps you bring at least some balance back to it. For me, it's my wife. She's always understood my passion, but at the same time she's helped me remember that there are other important things in life that you'll regret overlooking if you don't turn work off every now and then.

"Find great mentors. I've been lucky to have several over the years. My professors. My first creative director, Jim Mountjoy. My mother. My wife. For me, the best mentors have always shown you not just how to be better at your work but they've also stressed the importance of being a good person and keeping your ego in check.

"The Little Stuff:

"I get into work super early most days so that I have a couple hours to think before the chaos starts. I'm far more of a morning person than a night person.

"I spend at least half my time feeling like a hack. This way I stay driven to create better and better solutions for clients.

"I let the details bother me. There's nothing worse than creating something and then cringing when you look back at it a few months or years later because you overlooked some of the little things that could have made the work even better.

"Realize that the best solutions can come at the beginning or the end of the concepting process. Regardless of where they happen along the way, its important to keep pushing yourself to keep coming up with more work since you never know if you'll beat the ideas you already have."

—Doug Pedersen

Partner

"Like other insanely talented fine artists who find themselves in advertising, Doug Pedersen seems to process ad briefs visually, turning spoken thoughts into pictures even as he hears them. I suspect he does this without really thinking about it, which may be the secret to his success. Doug feels an advertising brief by translating it into a visual language that's meaningful to him personally. I think that's why his work makes such a strong connection with people who see it.

"One example is a series Doug did for Bell Canoe Works with his partner, the brilliant copywriter Heath Pochucha. Doug created the illustrations himself, and in them, he literally shows us what being on the water feels like. And he manages to nail just the right energy across the whole line of Bell products—from the serenity and solitude of Bell's touring canoes to the manic, swirling adrenaline of their class-five kayaks.

"Doug Pedersen's talent is that he constructs more than just an intellectual case for a brand. He uses his gift for art to make a motorcycle or a canoe into something much, much more than that. Something you might not have imagined yourself, but something you're real glad he did."

—Mike Lescarbeau, Chief Executive Officer, Carmichael Lynch

INSIGHTS FROM THE PROCESS CANVAS

Modesty yields a bit of shorthand. High-quality work belies the timeline presented here.

The ways creatives visualize time and space, particularly as parameters for a project, are fascinating.

Note the proportions of time here. Incubation and experimentation happen for as long as we'll allow. Deadlines demand an answer!

« "CALENDAR" MAGAZINE AD

Agency: Loeffler Ketchum Mountjoy, Charlotte, North Carolina **Creative Director:** Jim Mountjoy **Art Director:** Doug Pedersen **Creative Director/Writer:** Curtis Smith **Client:** North Carolina Travel and Tourism Division

NANCY RICE

FOUNDING PARTNER, FALLON McELLIGOTT RICE (MINNEAPOLIS, MINNESOTA)

©2009 Star Tribune, Minneapolis-St. Paul.

Nancy Rice working with her students at the Minneapolis College of Art and Design (MCAD).

FALLON McELLIGOTT RICE

N ancy Rice is a living legend and one of the most accomplished women in advertising history. She has held senior creative posts with agencies DDB Needham, Ogilvy & Mather and BBDO, among others. In 1981, she was a founding partner of Fallon McElligott Rice (now Fallon Worldwide), which was named Agency of the Year by *Advertising Age* only three years later.

In 1986, Rice was named Art Director of the Year by the Art Directors Club, and in 1989, her "Perception/Reality" campaign for *Rolling Stone* magazine was recognized as one of the ten best of the decade by *Adweek* and The One Club. In 1997, she became one of only six Americans to have her work documented in the *British Design and Art Direction Annual*. In 2006, she was inducted into the Art Directors Club Hall of Fame. Her work appears in countless award annuals. Did we mention she raised two children along the way?

Rice's focus turned to education as she was named worldwide creative director of Miami Ad School in 2001. Most recently, Rice served as coordinator of the advertising program at her alma mater, the Minneapolis College of Art and Design (MCAD).

Her long and productive career continues to inspire both students and professionals. Her secret? She likes to quote

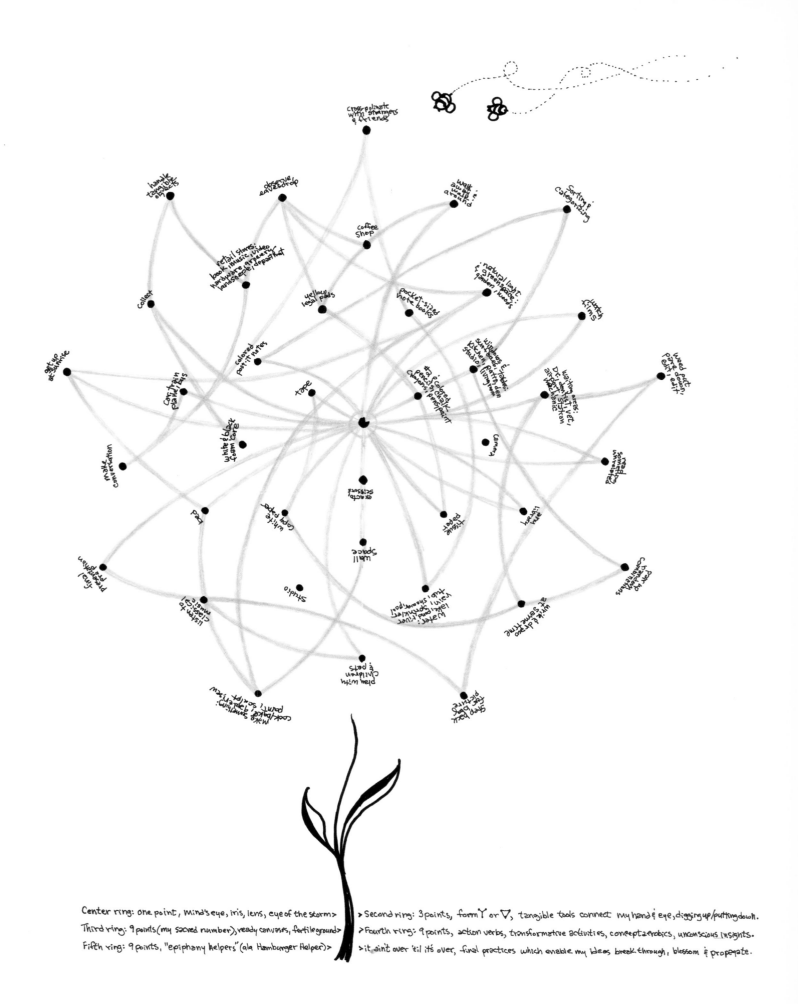

Center ring: one point, Mind's eye, iris, lens, eye of the storm>   >Second ring: 3 points, form Y or ∇, tangible tools connect my hand & eye, digging up/putting down.

Third ring: 9 points (my sacred number), ready canvases, fertile ground>   >Fourth ring: 9 points, action verbs, transformative activities, concept aerobics, unconscious insights.

Fifth ring: 9 points, "epiphany helpers" (ala Hamburger Helper)>   >it ain't over 'til it's over, final practices which enable my ideas break through, blossom & propagate.

The ability to both engage and disengage without fear at the appropriate moment is also tantamount to my creativity and outcome.

actress Ruth Gordon, who once said, "To be somebody, you must last."

Process

"My creative process has always been fluid, physical, instinctual, non-linear, varied each time. How do you draw that? Many elements come to play (with my muse and me) each time: actions, interactions, tangible tools, intervals of calm and chaos, all five senses, nature and geometry. The ability to both engage and disengage without fear at the appropriate moment is also tantamount to my creativity and outcome.

"The image that emerges from my process is circular (sacred to me) and is influenced, no doubt, by my Celtic roots! The plot points within the circle could have spoken to my mind's eye as fireworks, a wheel, a snowflake, a constellation, a pinwheel, a fountain or an airline route map—even the icing atop an elaborate dessert. But when I connected them, the geometry revealed a beautiful abstract flower. I gather inspiration from everywhere, so who was I to argue? I love the vigor, surprise and geometry of organizing, arranging and delivering an aromatic bouquet.

"It's both intimidating and inspiring to think about my personal creativity—my favorite combination!"

—Nancy Rice

Partner

"There's a story about a copywriter who once slammed his fist through Nancy Rice's office wall in a fit of frustration. The story is true. The writer in question had just learned a painful lesson: When working with Nancy, it's best to check your ego at the door. As everyone discovers sooner or later, she will not be intimidated, cajoled, coerced, threatened, lambasted, bribed, begged, bored or even complimented into accepting an idea—hers or yours—unless and until she's convinced of its rightness and originality.

"That's not to suggest that she was ever one to lose her temper or behave with anything less than grace and aplomb. On the contrary, when confronted with a bad idea, she had a simple and effective solution. Nancy would sit back from her drawing board and patiently wait until her sometimes exasperated creative partner was ready to return to the hard work and, yes, fun of making great advertising.

"Nancy has always had a way of keeping people honest, of getting the best from both herself and others. Sometimes when it meant serious sacrifice on her part. Sometimes, in fact, when it would have been far, far easier for pretty good rather than great. Compromise was just never part of her vocabulary."

—Tom McElligott, Founding Partner,
Fallon McElligott Rice

INSIGHTS FROM THE PROCESS CANVAS

Work environment contributes to process. "Natural light" and "wall space" can be key to an individual's productivity.

The visual metaphor here, a flower, connects to the idea that process is organic and must be nurtured in order to grow and blossom.

The tools creators use are beloved, specific and essential: The "yellow legal pad" might be perfect for one, while another might insist upon a journal with white, unlined pages.

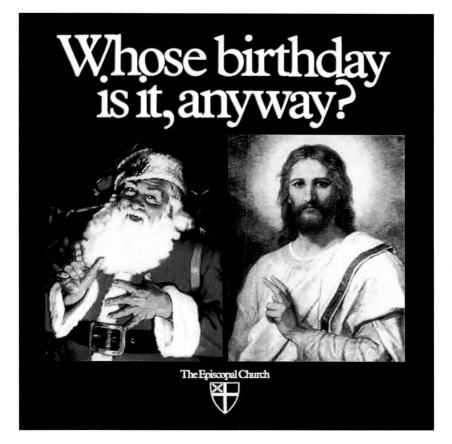

⌃ "WHOSE BIRTHDAY" AND "IF YOU THINK"
PRINT ADS

Agency: Fallon McElligott Rice, Minneapolis
Creative Director/Art Director: Nancy Rice
Creative Director/Writer: Tom McElligott **Client:**
The Episcopal Church

©1983 Church Ad Project

KEVIN RODDY

CHIEF CREATIVE OFFICER, BBH (NEW YORK, NEW YORK)

. . . .

B B H

After graduating from the University of Oregon, Kevin Roddy took a somewhat different path to a job in advertising copywriting. He avoided art school, ignored creative writing classes and, instead, jumped head-first into account management. But after years of writing nothing more creative than the occasional memo, Roddy made the transition to the creative department and never looked back. As a writer, he worked at several agencies on his way to BBH, including Fallon Worldwide and Cliff Freeman & Partners on a client roster that any creative would love... Little Caesars, Staples, Volvo, Coca-Cola, Electronic Arts, Timberland, *Time* and *Sports Illustrated* magazines, FOX Sports, FX Network. The big names.

In 2004, Roddy began his role as the executive creative director of BBH New York and, in that time, has helped the agency undergo a transformation. With Roddy's creative leadership,

For me, creativity is messy. It's random and unstructured and unpredictable. It's a lot of stopping and starting, experimenting and failing. It has tunnels, bridges, deep holes and high walls.

the agency has forged into new and broader creative territories, including, for starters, a television series on MTV for Axe called *The Gamekillers*; a YouTube sensation for Smirnoff Raw Tea called *Tea Partay*; and, most recently, the innovative launch of the new Oasis album, *Dig Out Your Soul*, via street musicians on the streets of New York City. As testimony to all this success, BBH New York recently named Roddy its Chief Creative Officer.

Boards magazine has twice ranked Roddy among the top three of its Top Ten Copywriters worldwide list, and he has won every major creative award in the world several times over. In fact, he's the only person in advertising ever to have won The One Show's Best of Show award twice. Roddy is also chairman of The One Club, one of the world's leading organizations to champion and promote creative excellence in advertising and design in all its forms. After all the awards and accolades, Roddy is still a writer, loving the start of another big idea.

Process

"For me, creativity is messy. It's random and unstructured and unpredictable. It's a lot of stopping and starting, experimenting and failing. It has tunnels, bridges, deep holes and

high walls. Did I mention holes and walls? It involves an incredible amount of questioning things and myself, and feeling ridiculously insecure. And I like it that way. I know there are people who want to control it because, at least in advertising, it has a defined purpose. But I always fight the urge those people have to understand and compartmentalize the creative process. I find comfort in not knowing where it's going. I need that time and space. I need to avoid structure to eventually find it. There are a lot of people who have intelligence and good sense, and I try to avoid those people because, in my creative process, they are not my friends. There is a time and place in advertising for creativity and good sense to connect but, for me, the two should never travel together on the same path."

—Kevin Roddy

Partner

"Kevin is an unusual creative director. He didn't start his advertising career in the creative department. He started out in management. He was an account handler.

"You could argue his late conversion to creativity should work against him.

"I actually think the opposite.

"His varied journey to the role of chief creative officer is partly what makes him great. It gives him perspective. It has made him a better creative thinker and leader.

"Experience is the foundation of creativity. Nothing can be created in a vacuum. It's impossible. Of course, experience doesn't make creative people great, but it does make it more likely.

"Also, to be a great creative leader, you have to have the respect of other creatives. And you have to know how to encourage people to fail. They have to have permission to get it wrong. And to let them know, whatever, they'll be supported. It's these qualities that make Kevin an outstanding creative leader.

"Which is great, because it certainly isn't his dress sense. I've never seen Kevin in anything but an oversized shirt, worn outside his blue jeans and always with an old pair of Timberland boots.

"What Kevin lacks in dress sense he makes up for in creative intuition."

—Sir John Hegarty, Co-Founder,
Bartle Bogle Hegarty, London

INSIGHTS FROM THE PROCESS CANVAS

The energy evident in this drawing is spectacular, a marvelous review of how people and ideas are in dynamic movement during process.

There's a story in each line. Seasoned professionals can look at this and know the nuance of making stuff happen.

Beauty, chaos, wit. There's the kind of arc you'd find in a movie script here, with a culminating moment that we know resulted in something big.

» *DIG OUT YOUR SOUL* ALBUM LAUNCH

Agency: BBH, New York **Chief Creative Officer:** Kevin Roddy **Creative Directors:** Pelle Sjönell, Calle Sjönell **Account Supervisor:** Chris Wollen **Producer:** Julian Katz; The Molloys, HSI Productions **Client:** Warner Music Group **Performers:** Meghan McGeary and Jim Bauer of DAGMAR

BBH teamed with Warner Music Group and New York City to reinvent the album launch for Oasis's seventh studio album, *Dig Out Your Soul*. The ambient campaign introduced new music on the streets of New York City, where band members taught street musicians—all members of the Metropolitan Transportation Authority's Music Under New York program—to play their songs for two weeks leading up to the album release in 2008.

« AXE DEODORANT'S "THE GAMEKILLERS"

Agency: BBH, New York **Executive Creative Director:** Kevin Roddy **Creative Director:** William Gelner **Art Director:** Jon Randazzo **Client:** Axe

"The Gamekillers" campaign played out in ads, ambient projects and on MTV. The Axe brand is positioned as more than a personal care product—it's a tool in the art of seduction. "The Gamekillers" concept offered young guys advice and insights for improving their "game" with girls by avoiding the archetypes that might stand in their way.

RYAN ROMERO

SENIOR INTERACTIVE COPYWRITER, PUBLICIS IN THE WEST (SEATTLE, WASHINGTON)

PUBLICIS IN THE WEST

Ryan Romero always wanted to be in advertising. As an eight-year-old, he thought the dialogue in the G.I. Joe commercials could be better.

His career began in Dallas, at a small traditional shop where he was the sole copywriter on accounts such as Taco Bueno and Community Coffee. His passion, however, lay in interactive. So, he made a bold move, and a short trip, across the

building to the offices of Tribal DDB in 2006. While there, he helped produce effervescent online work for Pepsi and Mountain Dew and learned to spell and pronounce Wojciechowski (his creative director's last name).

In 2008, Romero moved to Seattle, taking a job at Publicis in the West. His stated mission is "to deliver ideas that integrate traditional and digital advertising."

Romero lives with his beautiful wife, two dogs and a rapidly expanding collection of Dunny vinyl figures, flat stock posters and pop art. Romero is a Ducati motorcycle rider, disc golf player, tattoo canvas, citizen of Black Rock City and pretend grown up.

Process

"My creative process is constantly evolving, hard to pin down and, often, not a process at all. Sometimes it involves sitting

Ignore the clock. Ideas don't come on a schedule. They don't follow daylight savings time. It's like living in Mexico. Watch TV. Surf the Web. Play hookie and catch the matinee. Rot your brain – it makes it that much more fertile. Ask the damn question, already. It does no good in your head. WRITE SHIT DOWN! You will forget. Read something you hate. Look @ what's out there. Don't do it. It's been done. Scribble in the margins. Talk to yourself. Talk to your partner... about anything! If you think it, say it. Never preface an idea w/ "This is bad, but..." BULLSHIT! They're all good for something. Have a beer, this isn't church. Draw if you're a writer. Write if you're an AD. Take off your headphones. Talk to everyone within earshot. Refuse to use the phone. Talk face-to-face. Never buy a Blackberry. Quit the job that makes you carry one. Don't move to NYC to do great ads. Do them in Fresno. Shock everyone. Leave work early... come back @ 11... stay 'till 5. Never force an idea. Wait for it. When it comes, make it bigger. Forget budgets and clients. Never accept just one. They come in packs. Find his friends. Listen to your CD. Fight for your ideas. Never fear starting over. Be excited or your client won't be either. Fill the page, the whole page. And if you come up short, just make something up. You'll never regret your final line or last sketch. Well, probably not.

Logic doesn't work for me. Logic is what I come up with after the big idea is formed to explain to clients why it all makes sense.

in a small room with my partner drawing on white boards. Sometimes it's a headphones-on solo exercise in forced focus. Occasionally, an idea will make itself known while I'm walking to lunch, causing me to frantically type cryptic notes into my phone only to later wonder what the hell they mean.

"I've been told I should be more disciplined. That I should form a routine, write more lists or somehow better organize my thought process. But logic doesn't work for me. Logic is what I come up with after the big idea is formed to explain to clients why it all makes sense. 'Because it works,' doesn't convince as many people as you'd think.

"I've never been the type to throw out tons of ideas. My internal editor is impossible to turn off. Which means I need a partner who doesn't shut up. Bad ideas, random thoughts, strange music and anything outside my comfort zone are all necessary evils in my process. Make me hate something and I'll come back with a better idea. Give me a halfway acceptable thought and I get lazy. Maybe I'm just confrontational.

"In the end, I believe. I have to.

"I come in every day and work for the big idea, but it shows up on its own schedule. So, I have to have faith it will emerge eventually and hope to hell it's not too late when it does."

—Ryan Romero

Partner

"I can't imagine putting the mind of Ryan Romero on paper. You really have to experience it. For me, being his partner was easy, although his process was to go against a process.

"Anytime we'd sit and concept, we'd never let the day-to-day bullshit hold us up, whether it was agency politics or personal matters. We had a vibe: sitting in front of each other, starting to think and flow. This was our starting point: What is the problem or main objective? Then, from there, we came up with solutions using whatever approach felt right. There was not a predictable pattern. But we did always try to generate as many ideas as possible, because one was never good enough.

"The great thing about working with Ryan was our dynamic. When we had great ideas, we let each other know. And when we had awful ideas, we let each other know that, too. That is what makes a great team. I think Ryan pushes people to get the best out of them. He makes them think and explore parts of their mind they might not have on their own. And when you see Ryan, you will always catch him carrying his black book full of ideas."

—Brandy Cole, Senior Art Director,
Tribal DDB, Dallas

INSIGHTS FROM THE PROCESS CANVAS

The imperative statements here are marks of conviction. Every sentence is based on a lesson learned firsthand.

Mentoring is an agency ritual. Always listen. Never stop being a student.

LUKE SULLIVAN

GROUP CREATIVE DIRECTOR, GSD&M (AUSTIN, TEXAS)

Luke Sullivan is a rock star. Students of the craft know him from his beloved book, *Hey Whipple, Squeeze This*, dog-eared copies of which can be found at every ad school around the world. When he speaks to classes, he insists that language and words mean something. "Writers have to love the act of writing," he says. To illustrate that point: Journals that he has filled over the years line the walls of his home study, a testament to his love for the craft.

He began his career as the understudy to the famed Tom McElligott at Bozell & Jacobs in Minneapolis, where, he says, McElligott "helped teach me to write, to build friction into your work so that your message doesn't just lie there, but requires something of you."

A ten-year stint at the Minneapolis agency Fallon McElligott Rice propelled him to industry fame. He also served as vice

LUKE SULLIVAN

STRATEGY: Usually, I reserve the top of the first page of the first tablet for a simple, flat-footed statement of what my ad has to communicate. I just say it, flat: "This outboard engine is reliable and fast." Boom.

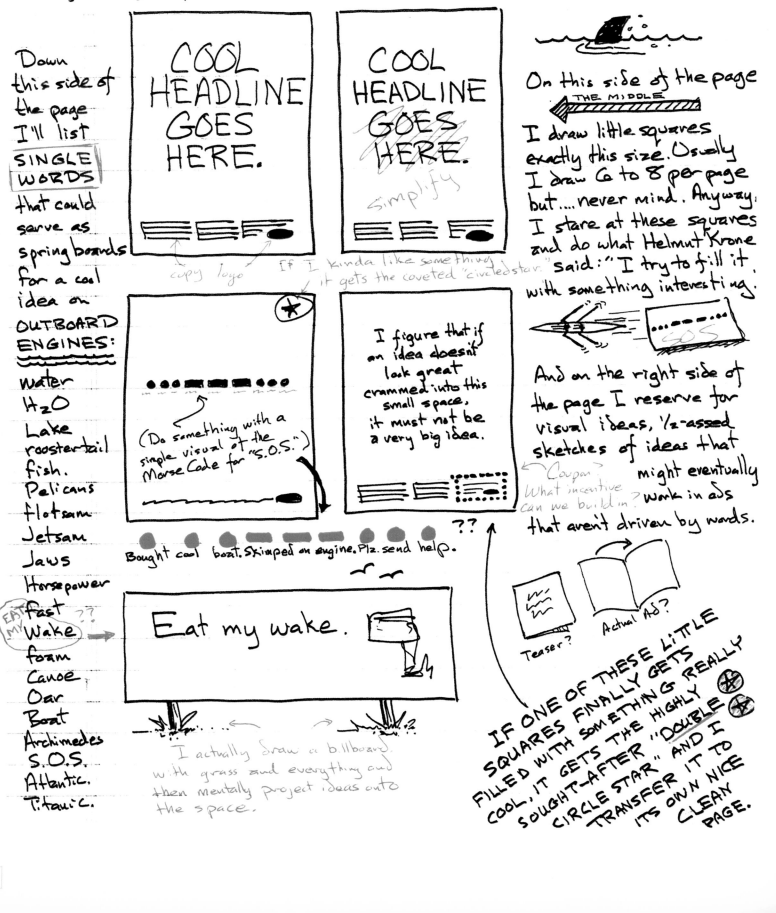

Down this side of the page I'll list SINGLE WORDS that could serve as springboards for a cool idea on OUTBOARD ENGINES:

water
H₂O
Lake
roostertail
fish.
Pelicans
flotsam
Jetsam
Jaws
Horsepower
fast ??
Wake
foam
Canoe
Oar
Boat
Archimedes
S.O.S.
Atlantic
Titanic.

EAT MY

COOL HEADLINE GOES HERE.

copy logo

If I kinda like something, it gets the coveted "circled star."

(Do something with a simple visual of the Morse Code for "S.O.S.")

COOL HEADLINE GOES HERE.
simplify

I figure that if an idea doesn't look great crammed into this small space, it must not be a very big idea.

Bought cool boat. Skimped on engine. Plz. send help. ??

Eat my wake.

I actually draw a billboard with grass and everything and then mentally project ideas onto the space.

On this side of the page
THE MIDDLE
I draw little squares exactly this size. Usually I draw 6 to 8 per page but.....never mind. Anyway. I stare at these squares and do what Helmut Krone said: "I try to fill it with something interesting."

SOS

And on the right side of the page I reserve for visual ideas, ½-assed sketches of ideas that
Coupon?
What incentive can we build in? might eventually work in ads that aren't driven by words.

Teaser?   Actual Ad?

IF ONE OF THESE LITTLE SQUARES FINALLY GETS FILLED WITH SOMETHING REALLY COOL, IT GETS THE HIGHLY SOUGHT-AFTER "DOUBLE CIRCLE STAR" AND I TRANSFER IT TO ITS OWN NICE CLEAN PAGE.

Then I stare at that little white space. I just stare. And I try to fill it with something interesting.

president of The Martin Agency in Richmond, Virginia, working alongside agency lead Mike Hughes. Hughes, according to Sullivan, "taught me how important it is to be a nice person in this business. He is a kind-hearted soul, and you work your tail off for him because you love him so much."

In the 1990s, Sullivan was named chief creative officer of Atlanta's WestWayne. After four years there, he moved to Austin. Today, he is group creative head at GSD&M.

The quality of Sullivan's work makes the Whipple book worth reading and has earned him credibility among young people and the industry. He's been named to *Adweek*'s list of the top ten copywriters in America twice. He's won dozens of topflight awards from The One Show, Cannes Lions, *Communication Arts*, and London's D&AD show. The brands that bear his mark—among them AT&T, Miller Lite, United Airlines, Lee Jeans and Ralston Purina, as well as Porsche, BMW and Maserati—offer a cross-section of American life.

Process

(Reprinted from "How to Write a Newspaper Ad," Newspaper Association of America, www.nna.org.)

"I draw a little blank white square. About one inch wide, two inches deep. I figure if I can't get my idea inside of that small space, it must not be a very big idea and it's only going to look worse filling up a 13" x 21" newspaper page.

"Then I stare at that little white space. I just stare. And I try to fill it with something interesting. Unfailingly, the first one hundred ideas that I draw inside that little white square are awful little things.

"That's when it starts: a special sort of chest-splitting panic known only to people whose work is produced on a deadline and appears in forums as public as the newspaper.

"To deal with this horror, mature writers pour another cup of coffee and buckle in. I, however, remember that the movie *Memento* just opened and sneak out of the agency leaving a Post-it note ('at focus group, have cell phone') stuck on the desk, next to my cell phone.

"After I come back from the movie, Idea #101 comes along. It's not great, but it's 'pretty good.' Braced with this small victory, I change gears. If I've been thinking verbally, I switch to visual.

"Finally, my pen starts moving. But upon review, Ideas #102 through #130 all stink, and I go home in despair. The next day or maybe the next week I discover Idea #101 clicks like a Lego into Idea #131.

"'Wow,' I think. 'It's not bad.' And the anvil that has been on my chest since the day I started writing, slides off."

—Luke Sullivan

Partner

"Luke and I worked together as partners quite early in our careers, and I was impressed by his early ability to do it all: strategic thinking, copywriting, art direction, planning (before it was called planning), media thinking and, of course, writing best-selling advertising novels on company time. Luke is the consummate writer in that he has learned to think visually before thinking verbally."

—Bob Barrie, Co-Founder/Art Director,
Barrie D'Rozario Murphy, Minneapolis

INSIGHTS FROM THE PROCESS CANVAS

The case study is a powerful way to illustrate how process unfolds. The professional, the author, the teacher shares what he knows.

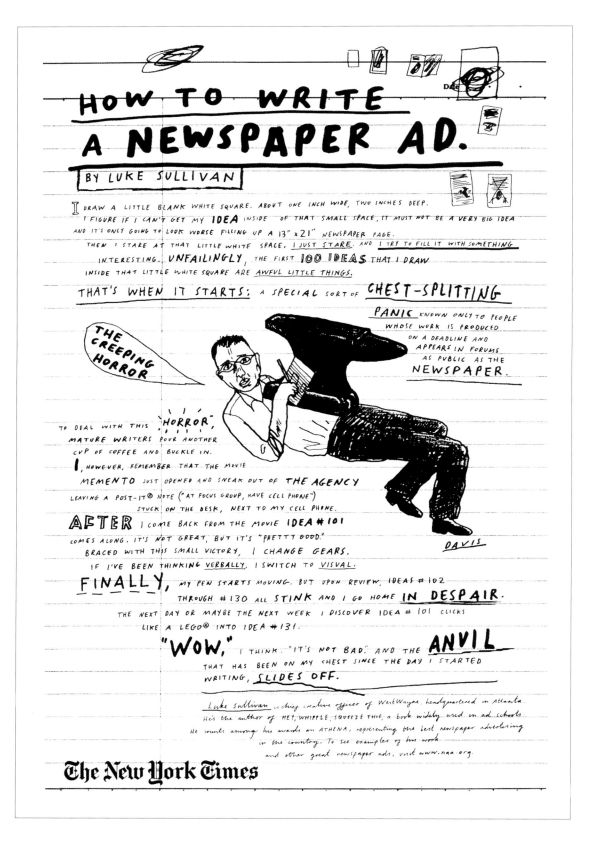

⌃ "HOW TO WRITE A NEWSPAPER AD"

Creative Director/Art Director: Luke Sullivan
Creative Director/Writer: Luke Sullivan
Client: Newspaper Advertising Association

DAVID SWOPE

SENIOR ART DIRECTOR, McCANN ERICKSON; CREATIVE DIRECTOR/ART DIRECTOR,
SWOPE CREATIVE (SAN FRANCISCO, CALIFORNIA)

D avid Swope is the busiest guy on the West Coast. He's enjoyed a bright career with just about every agency in San Francisco. He's turned Swope Creative into a go-to boutique that produces work for a range of clients and causes. And his day job happens to be senior art director at McCann Erickson, where he brings a strategic, media-agnostic view of advertising to the agency table.

Swope has worked with a range of clients from California Cheese to Hewlett-Packard, from FOX Sports to *Star Wars*. He's had plenty of clients whose names ended in ".com." He's had to sell "infrastructure management solutions." Three times. Despite this, his work has been recognized by the Clios, Cannes Lions, *Graphis*, *Communication Arts*, the OBIEs, the Emmys, the Tellys, the ADDYs, the San Francisco Show, *Lürzer's Archive*, *Creativity* and *Print*.

I usually start by asking: Why is the brief wrong?

In 2006, Swope took on global warming with CooltheWorld.org. In 2009, he helped La Leche League of Marin get the message out to support breastfeeding acceptance. His other socially-responsible client experience includes "Flex Your Power" for California Energy Efficiency and Conservation, ZAP Electric Vehicles, Goodwill, the Long Now Foundation, Marin farmers' markets, Coral Reef Alliance and World War II Research & Preservation Society. He believes not all advertising is evil. And he drives a hybrid.

Process

"I usually start by asking: Why is the brief wrong? Because it almost always is. Most creative briefs cannot lead to good advertising unless they are developed with input from creatives—or at least a planner with some creative bones (a British accent is helpful). A fresh brief will lead to fresh ideas. As long as you have enough time to do it right.

"It's like the old story about cows that are let out of a barn. The ones who stop at the first grass they come across end up chewing well-trod bits of weeds and muddy tufts. The more adventurous cows who make it past the first (or second) pastures find the good, deep, tasty stuff. Just don't go too far and become roadkill.

"Of course, obstacles are everywhere. No budget. Weak coffee. A creative partner who's been beaten down. Focus groups. The client's wife. They all form a virtually impenetrable wall separating you from success. And then there's the problem that Crispin already did whatever you're thinking of doing.

"The painful reality is that this business is not just about finding the Big Idea. It's just as important to sell the Big Idea. So, unless you have the right attitude, advertising will kill you. For every one hundred ideas you have, it's just a fact of life that ninety-nine of your babies will die. You have to be completely okay with rejection from your partner, the creative director, the account team and the client. And if somehow your idea gets produced? Well, congratulations. Now you can be rejected by the consumer.

"The bottom line: Be Teflon. Don't let failure stick—smile and roll with it. Because when it comes to getting to the Big Idea, if you don't enjoy the journey, you'll never make it to the destination."

—David Swope

Partner

"I have worked with David on more than thirty projects.

"Some have been small, quick shoots. Others have been major campaigns for some of the largest companies in the world.

"Regardless of the size of the job, David always has enthusiasm and an 'anything is possible' attitude. His positive energy is contagious. His method centers around being open-minded, tenacious, focused and having a healthy amount of curiosity.

"As the photographer, I am usually consulted once an idea has been developed and sold to the client. Generally, David or the ad agency's art buyer tells me the concept or message of the photos. However, David always leaves room for us to go beyond the comp/layout while still honoring the original message. The basic guideline is, do what will make the strongest ad. He is driven by this credo. The reality is, making mediocre work is a soul (and business) killer.

"On set or location, David makes certain we get the original assignment photographed and we go further to capture the best of the other possibilities. Sometimes, this may require David doing a quick sketch (on set) to show me yet a new idea that just developed through watching me shoot. This sketch may create other ideas from me that he didn't consider. It's part of the creative process and how an original 'idea' gets to a healthy, engaging visual.

"Most of the time, the newer ideas are what get produced and win awards."

—Curtis Myers, Photographer,
San Francisco

INSIGHTS FROM THE PROCESS CANVAS

That brick wall is big and bad. It keeps getting in the way before it's finally overcome.

Some personalities may be obstacles within the creative feedback loop: the client's wife, the jaded writer, other pros.

"Learn" is an important term. Do your research, yes, but don't forget to learn.

Global Warming is a Choice.

Flex your POWER.ORG

⌃ "FLOOD" POSTER

Agencies: McGuire & Co.; Brainchild Creative, San Francisco **Campaign Director:** Walter McGuire **Concept and Copy:** Jef Loeb **Art Director:** David Swope **Photographer:** Curtis Myers **Client:** Flex Your Power

RANDY TATUM

VICE PRESIDENT/GROUP CREATIVE DIRECTOR, MARTIN | WILLIAMS (MINNEAPOLIS, MINNESOTA)

© 2010 Sean Kennedy Santos

Randy Tatum feels lucky. He spent a couple of years in Chicago and a nice ten-year run at Carmichael Lynch in Minneapolis before making the switch to a Martin | Williams vice-presidency and creative director post. Over his career, he's created work for brands including Harley-Davidson Motorcycles and MotorClothes, IKEA, Coca-Cola, Target, Tractor Supply Company, A.G. Edwards, Northwest Airlines and Bolla Wines, to name a few.

He's won a few awards, too: Cannes Lions, Effies, *Communications Arts*, The One Show, D&AD, the MPA Kellys, Clios, *Adweek*'s Best and his personal favorite, ESPN's inclusion of his TV spot "Chevy Snowstorm" as one of the top ten Michael Jordan TV commercials ever produced.

If lucky means more than a decade of hard work, magic with light and photos, a way with clients and partners and

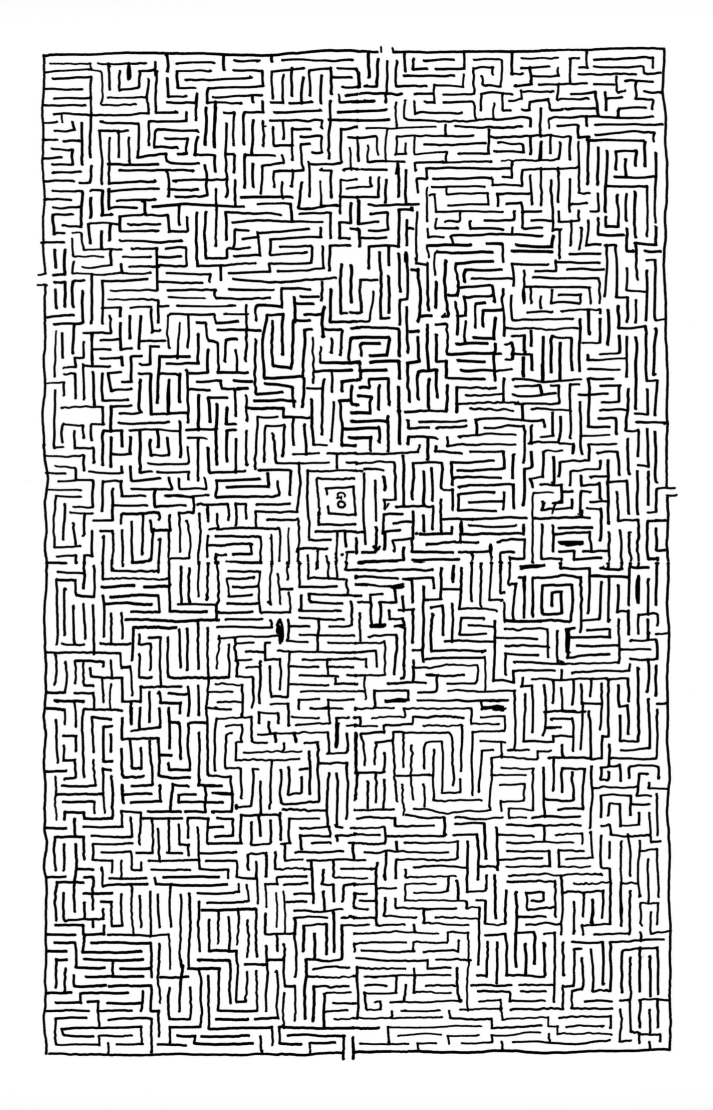

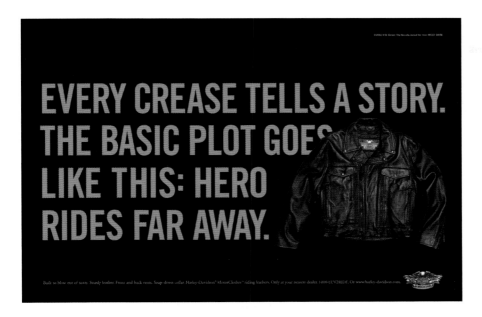

« "EVERY CREASE" MAGAZINE AD

Agency: Martin|Williams, Minneapolis
Creative Director: Jim Nelson **Art Director:**
Randy Tatum **Writer:** Tom Camp **Photographer:**
Shawn Michienzi **Client:** Harley-Davidson
MotorClothes

colleagues, and a surefire designer's eye, then Tatum's been so. For now, let's just say he's earned his corner office.

Process

"Here's how it happens:

"It starts off with a few ideas that you know are children that have ten fingers and ten toes but possess no real motor skills. But 'Hey, no worries, we just got going,' you say. 'We'll come up with something tomorrow. Let's play pool.' Then it all goes dark. And the terrifying realization that it's finally, officially over—you're done, you've got nothing, all the ideas are gone, and you'll be turning in your club membership card—firmly takes hold in the insect portion of your brain. That lasts anywhere from forty-eight to seventy-two hours. It's horrible. The worst. Then something happens. You see something. Your partner says something. Somebody thinks something. And the beautiful chase begins again for the Idea.

"And that's what it is all about."

—Randy Tatum

Partner

"The secret of creative genius is that it really isn't genius—it's perseverance. Most people think it's the 'aha' moments that hit you in the shower that turn into Gold Lions at Cannes. If that were true, we'd have a world full of better smelling creatives.

"Randy Tatum is part of the shortlist I've come across who can conjure up and then capture the creative process over and over. Watching Randy continually bag the big idea throughout his career has motivated me and the teams around him to keep

pushing, to never settle, to peek under every rock—until you find a gem.

"The process is organic, frenetic, layered and unpredictable. It takes throwing hundreds of ideas up on the wall to find one or two good enough to pursue. It takes a rare discipline to let go of good, to continue the search for gold.

"Simply put, Randy is a maniac. I've seen him kill more good ideas then the average art director sees in his life. And that level of crazy—or passion—is what it takes. It's a labor of love. Hacking away at good ideas until only the great remain.

"Nurturing those solid ideas is where the fun of creating comes in. You have these little idea sprouts… now how do you grow them into sustainable, self-sufficient concepts? What personality do you give them? What kind of voice will it have? Only by trial and error, risk and reward, do the best ideas become great ads. That ability to keep pushing through the clutter separates the Randys from the rest."

—Kathy Umland, Vice President/
Director of Creative Operations,
Martin|Williams, Minneapolis

INSIGHTS FROM THE PROCESS CANVAS

"Go" is where it starts. Why is that sometimes the hard part?

The complexity of the process is complete with obstacles and multiple paths to a solution.

31° Fahrenheit

98.6° Fahrenheit

NOW YOU CAN RIDE THROUGH ANYTHING. Introducing Harley-Davidson® FXRG® riding gear. The brainchild of 100 years on the road. An integrated system only riders could design. Head-to-toe comfort. And the function to ride far, warm and dry. The all-conditions revolution is here. Get to your H-D dealer and be a part of it. www.harley-davidson.com.

⌃ "FAHRENHEIT" MAGAZINE AD

Agency: Martin│Williams, Minneapolis
Creative Director/Art Director: Randy Tatum **Writer:** Eric Sorensen **Client:** Harley-Davidson MotorClothes

DEACON WEBSTER

FOUNDER/CHIEF CREATIVE OFFICER, WALRUS (NEW YORK, NEW YORK)

WALRUS

A great name that will help fans and clients follow your progress? Check. Small, hot-shop creative experience that earns you a reputation for the offbeat? Check. A hip Union Square office (that you own) with built-in sense of humor and brave clients? Check. In the creative world, Deacon Webster pretty much has it made.

After graduating from college in 1995, Webster began his career as a writer at Mad Dogs & Englishmen in New York doing award-winning work for accounts such as Moviefone, Yoo-Hoo, Road Runner High Speed Online and Friends of Animals. He was a quick study. He founded the Mad Dogs San Francisco office in 2000 before bouncing back to the New York office to become executive creative director two years later.

Walrus, a nimble agency Webster founded five years ago after Mad Dogs shuttered, does a little of everything. Its clients include *Howard Stern On Demand*, *The Economist*, Major League Baseball, Grand Marnier, Lucky Brand Jeans and Liz Claiborne. Clients have come to expect the unexpected from Walrus.

To date, Webster's work has been recognized by The One Show, D&AD, the Art Directors Club, *Communication Arts* and

I. CREATIVE BRIEFING
↓

1. Write 3 or 4 ideas down while briefer is talking.

2. Decide that at least 2 of these ideas are amazing and that the problem is solved.

3. Ask questions designed to reinforce validity of aforementioned brilliant ideas.

4. Draw up ideas upon returning to desk.

5. Go home / go to bed.

6. Get back to work, see ideas on desk — realize they're complete crap.

II. CONCEPTING

1. BRIEF DISSECTION
a) "What are they looking for?"
b) "Is that doable?"
c) If so, is it doable well?
d) If not, what is it trying to accomplish?
e) Is this doable?

Basically I try and figure out the agendas of everyone involved with the brief, and how it affects the brief. Is this brief recommending print because it's cheap, because they've always done print, or because of something else. I try and get every bit of information I can so I can figure out the mindset of the people I'll be presenting to.

2. COFFEE. GET SOME. DRAW LITTLE SQUARES. If it's a print assignment I draw lots of these:

Sometimes I practice drawing the product or logo (you know, for later when I have an idea).

GRAND MARNIER BOTTLES ARE HARD:
This bit is the weird part
BETTER

2A. WRITE A FEW TAGLINES
a) If it's not pie, then who wants it?
What could life be life without pie?
Pie makes everyone look good.

B) Try and work back from the tagline.
(Picture of Hitler eating cake greedily)
(Lyrics to "Sing-a-song of six pence" with the word "pie" replaced with "calzone")
(Hitler in "kiss the cook" apron holding a piping apple pie. Angelic back lighting makes him look wholesome)

C) Refill coffee. Surf internet. Pace. Go home go to bed.
— You Tube
— News Today
— ESPN
— Porn

This is a part of the process I call "bitching and moaning" which is essentially just procrastination. Planners & Acct. people HATE this.

3. Try getting up really early and working. Good ideas come at 5:30 AM. Drink coffee.

4. Try laying a few ideas out. Sometimes this leads to new ideas other times it reveals big problems — like the fact that your idea is really complicated.

5. Coffee

6. SWITCH MEDIA — Sometimes I'll pick a lovely typeface, and set it white on black and just write headlines. This doesn't mean I'm looking for a headline ad — but somehow it helps me put forth simple notions quickly.

Occasionally I'll switch off the computer and move to paper which is also refreshing. Pen to pencil... gives a different aesthetic. Dick may lead to something. Maybe... House letters is a god time waster. I draw a lot of arrows with a pencil. Trend would have a field day with this.

7. GO SOMEWHERE. Coffee shop, Barnes & Noble, Park. A change of scene is always nice & refreshing. Especially if it's a place that sells coffee.

8. Look at books. Design, art, whatever. It's good to see how other people are expressing ideas.

9. Inevitably the only thing that forces me to concentrate fully on a problem is a looming deadline. If I've got time, I'm usually procrastinating.

10. Present work. You learn a lot by presenting:
— What's funny
— What makes sense
— What they aren't looking for.
— What's complicated

I pay a lot of attention to initial reactions — meaning as I read it. Client comments from 4 or 5 people — not so much because they. Aren't reacting emotionally anymore — it becomes posturing for the meeting. That's not to say I don't listen, but beyond "I don't like it," it's hard to get too much direction from large groups because they're being way too scientific.

Head nods, laughter, scowls, note taking, stone faces

11. Repeat.

4. I also like ads that lie, blatantly. If I'm stuck, I'll just make some claim up and try to validate it. If it's outrageous enough it can be really funny.
5. Charts / graphs — they always have a few. Try a few.

Some words I like: Leviathan, turnip, hilarious, dugong, budgie, gravy boat, mallet, fern

> Food is funny (especially meats) (but not in food ads)
3. I also have a list of words that I like to get into ads. Sometimes I'll try and work an idea around getting this word in.

A COUPLE OF OTHER TRICKS:
1. I keep a mental list of things I think are funny. Some are funny as words. Some are funny as pictures. — Rutabaga. Some are funny as pictures:

Some are funny as a picture with words:
Chow-Chow, Ham, Spatula, Grape

Pie makes everyone look good!

This bit off ASP can be quite amusing as a procrastination tool/toy

I drew this with a Pilot fineliner — which is best for fineliners (I guess that)

We made some cool "concepting pads" at the office that have a square printed on them so you don't have to draw it. At the bottom of each page it says "a tree died for this idea" gotta love pressure.

MAGIC AD FRAME!!!
BETTER
2D TESSERACT
A BAD ONE

Pen of choice: Uniball Vision Fine. Saddam Hussein had one of these when Dan Rather interviewed him pre-invasion. I now call it "the pen of evil" with this pen, I draw lots of these:

When a campaign finally goes live, I get really anxious, but in a good way. It's kind of like when you get all excited about giving somebody a present and you can't wait for them to open it.

the Clios. A stack of awards and honors to validate a unique portfolio of work? Check.

Process

"Each new assignment is like a big, complex puzzle that has to be solved in its own way, but basically it always boils down to the same thing: 'How do we say this without making people think we're just some annoying ad?' When a campaign finally goes live, I get really anxious, but in a good way. It's kind of like

⌃ "SQUIRRELS" AMBIENT MEDIA

Agency: Mad Dogs & Englishmen, New York
Creative Director: Dave Cook **Art Director:** Darren Lim **Writer:** Deacon Webster **Client:** Friends of Animals

when you get all excited about giving somebody a present and you can't wait for them to open it. Rationally, I'm highly confident that it's going to be great, but there's always this glimmer of doubt. It's as if there's this cranky, little, naysayer gnome that lives in my head and says stuff like, 'That is the STUPIDEST thing I've ever heard,' and 'Now you've done it, they're FINALLY going to figure out that you're really just a janitor.' Then, of course, it all goes well and the gnome goes into hiding for a day or two until the next campaign comes around."

—Deacon Webster

Partner

"Deacon. What goes on in that mind of his? He sits staring at a layout pad, Sharpie in hand… rarely in front of a computer, if I remember correctly. His expression always seems quite serious… deeply concerned… like something profound is bothering him… niggling him. At this point he could be thinking anything. The meaning of life? How a gourd can grow so large? What is wrong with the New York Jets' offense? Every few minutes he may spontaneously begin nodding, then the long sigh, and silence again. He's supposedly a writer, but he never seems to write much. He just draws strange caricatures, oddities, doodles… pages and pages of these, one after the other. He mutters… he scratches an ear. An hour passes. His mind is now journeying, he's in transit, somewhere in the middle of India, or wandering around inside his mother's uterus… then… all of a sudden… a broad satisfied grin slowly stretches its way across his weathered, gentle face, like he just solved the *New York Times*' Friday crossword puzzle. It's over. He has it. He's done it. It? What is it? Who is this madman? What kind of a name is Deacon anyway?"

—Nick Cohen, Executive Creative Director, Wieden+Kennedy, Shanghai, China

INSIGHTS FROM THE PROCESS CANVAS

Details, notes in margins: a description of a favorite pen, the curve of beautiful bottles, funny lists. The little things are big.

Presentation of an idea is an opportunity to learn and to refine. Reactions and feedback are valuable.

CHAPTER FOUR
PROCESS IS POWERFUL

Advertising creativity represents a wondrous intersection of art and commerce, as evidenced by the compelling collection of work in this book. Although some might suggest that the two should never mix, a well-conceived ad can convey ideas and emotion and can move people to act—qualities that are often celebrated in the works of fine and performing artists. We also argue that advertising, when considered as an art form, can be as strong a cultural force as anything housed in a museum, staged on Broadway or touring live in concert. That doesn't make advertising better, of course, but it does make it important. When it is done right, advertising is as worthy of our admiration and respect as a traditional work of art. It's also deserving of careful examination and study.

The creative professionals who develop big ideas are advertising's artists in residence. They are quite prolific and their pieces are well known, but the creators don't sign them in the bottom corner. Whether it's a Super Bowl spot or the largest billboard in Times Square, we believe the real value of all great advertising is rooted in the process that produced it. Creative directors, art directors and writers understand how their minds work and constantly adapt their own thinking to meet the demands of the job. This brain trust is the power that sustains the industry and much of the world's economy. And that makes these people advertising's most valuable resource. We thought you'd enjoy getting to know them (and learning from them) the way we do every day.

In chapter three, you met thirty-six bright creatives from the advertising world. You read about their backgrounds and their achievements, and you saw samples of their work. They spoke to you about their process. You also heard from their colleagues, who described what it's like to work with them. But perhaps the greatest moments of discovery were found in their drawings, which show the process on paper. We find these illustrations fascinating and full of meaning. They say so many things that words can't express.

In this chapter, we'll review those remarkable drawings and explain how they help us better understand the nature of advertising creativity. We'll begin by analyzing the visual characteristics of the illustrations themselves. Then we'll discuss several dimensions of the creative process that these illustrations collectively reveal to us.

PROCESS ILLUSTRATED: VISUALIZING THE INVISIBLE

How can I draw something I can't see? It's a fair question. It's one that no doubt occurred to many of the people whose drawings are featured in this book. If you've ever imagined what heaven looks like or dreamed a mental picture of the perfect mate, then you know that the mind can build images of things we've never seen. The imagination fills in visual gaps all the time.

The creative professionals who develop big ideas are advertising's artists in residence.

But is the creative process in advertising really so invisible? Sure, there's stuff happening in the brain that we're not able to directly observe. However, a lot of the work invested in the discovery of a new idea happens outside the brain and in the physical realm. Maybe there's library research, or testing the product, or consulting with experts to get their opinions—all very visible activities.

The drawings in chapter three show us the process as conceptualized by people who use it every day on the job. They are based on experience—however the process feels, unfolds, stops, starts again and ultimately resolves itself. They incorporate all kinds of variables that help us better understand how the process works (we'll discuss these later as "dimensions" of the creative process). They truly are works of art.

The creative process is a uniquely human experience. When asked to describe that process, people rely upon their memories (some more recent, some more distant) to reconstruct the phenomenon. (We know this from our own experiences conducting in-depth interviews with creative professionals.) The same effort to reconstruct the phenomenon via memory is triggered when one attempts to visualize the process. In 1998, Danish researcher Steen F. Larsen proposed a set of descriptive categories that can be used to evaluate visual elements of memories. We'll use a few of Larsen's terminologies along with a few of our own to discuss some of the most prominent visual characteristics of the process drawings.

Spatial Relationships

One way to evaluate a drawing is to note how elements occupy the space on a page. The size or relative scale of objects and the use of empty or negative space are common examples of spatial relationships that can communicate information to the viewer.

Some contributors used size to indicate the importance of a specific part of their process, or how much time and effort it demands:

> **ROSS CHOWLES (page 45):** The relative size of the bathtub to all other pictures on the page communicates the belief that allowing information to "sit with you" for a while is a crucial step towards idea generation.

> **RACHEL HOWALD (page 91):** Substantial periods of writing are followed by the impulse to throw all the work away and to start over again. The most frenetic writing is done closest to the achievement of the solution.

> **IAN COHEN (page 52):** Each step in the process is equally important for finding the idea. Don't shortchange any one of them.

In some cases, filling the entire page with visuals or words made a powerful statement:

> **DUSTIN BALLARD (page 38):** "Big ideas" emerge from limitless possibilities.

> **RYAN ROMERO (page 138):** "Fill the page, the whole page." There's so much advice to offer anyone who wants to do this job right. He'll pack in as much of it as possible in the space available, but this is just a start.

Ross Chowles

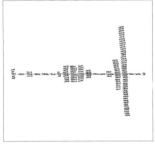

Rachel Howald

Ian Cohen

Dustin Ballard

Ryan Romero

Glenn Cole

Jim Mountjoy

Tom Christmann

Janet Kestin/Nancy Vonk

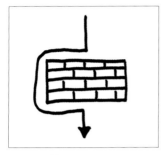

Kevin Roddy

David Swope

Matthew Barber

Luke Sullivan

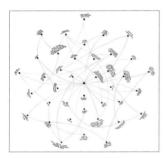

Nancy Rice

Vast, empty spaces on the page also served important functions:

GLENN COLE (page 56): The eye is immediately drawn to the center of the page, where a singular, simple statement of his creative philosophy is made. Nothing else is important enough to share the same space.

JIM MOUNTJOY (page 122): The negative space creates a visual "funnel," communicating the distillation of a powerful idea from a well-written creative brief.

What was a key variable, obstacle, factor or resource that influences how the process works? It was often the first element of the drawing to catch the eye:

TOM CHRISTMANN (page 49): The lengthy URL list indicates the importance of online material as a source of inspiration.

JANET KESTIN/NANCY VONK (page 103): The process always begins with a problem to solve. The team "that fits" surrounds it and starts proposing solutions.

KEVIN RODDY (page 134), DAVID SWOPE (page 145): The "brick wall" represents a variety of obstacles that can block the process at different points. These obstacles can feel monumental but must be overcome.

Color

We provided contributors with a black Sharpie marker and a blank canvas to accommodate their process drawings. Several took the opportunity to add color to their illustrations as a means for highlighting elements or to show how they related to each other.

Color was used as a cue for specific identification:

MATTHEW BARBER (page 41): The rings haphazardly scattered across the page are the unmistakable color of coffee and represent both a habit and a tool characteristic of his process.

Isolated flashes of color set particular elements apart from others and underscored their importance to the process:

LUKE SULLIVAN (page 141): His name is there in bold, red capital letters at the top of the page, as if to say, "This is my process and I take ownership of it." An industry veteran, he has much invested in it, but also the generosity to share it with the rest of us.

Color also showed the relationship and interplay between elements of the process:

NANCY RICE (page 130): This is a process that is informed by work environment, ritual, tools, philosophy and experience. Their interdependence is captured with an art director's favorite: non-repro blue.

Vividness/Clarity

Several of the drawings were quite simple yet visually powerful in summarizing the essence of an individual's creative process. Rather than revealing it using a step-by-step approach, these illustrations offered the pathway to ideas in shorthand form.

SILVER CUELLAR (page 60): "I put my head on a page and see what sticks," Cuellar states plainly. There's great confidence here that good ideas will flow when one is wholeheartedly and personally invested in the process, when you put yourself into the work.

JIM HAVEN (page 79): For Haven, everything around him informs creative thinking, perhaps involuntarily. The key is to keep the mind open and receptive to all input and influences.

DAVID HORRIDGE (page 87): As founder of his own shop and a former freelancer, Horridge is no doubt accustomed to a great deal of solitary work and expresses its importance to the process here. Finding a quiet place can facilitate deep focus on a problem and all possible solutions.

Detail

In visualizing their creative process, many of our contributors felt compelled to capture it in as much detail as possible in order to make it truly personal. These drawings incorporated many habits, secrets and favorite techniques, and lots of personal advice, among other gems. Additionally, the most detailed drawings usually offered a sense of the order in which the process occurs. It was fun to discover how individuals bring their own unique approaches to the same professional task.

ANDY AZULA (page 30): Azula is always moving and doing. His process seems to rely on constant action and productivity. Even when he's not working (surfing the 'net) he's working ("front-loading" his day).

DANNY GREGORY (page 72): Creativity is a habit, according to Gregory. "You have to keep your creative muscles exercised," he insists. He challenges himself to make something every day. Being creative outside the office helps prepare him to be creative-on-demand when necessary.

DAVID T. JONES (page 95): With respect to a creative process, Jones claims he doesn't have one, unless you count the "rough, odd journey from assignment to idea." Then he takes us through it: that process that isn't a process. Call it what you will, it works.

SIMON MAINWARING (page 115): Mainwaring is the man with all the plans. His process is essentially a library of problem-solving protocols. He can look at any problem and match it with a variety of effective techniques to generate a solution. In fact, he suggests that "the problem is the solution," or that truly understanding a problem is the key to solving it.

DEACON WEBSTER (page 153): There's a strong sense of curiosity throughout Webster's creative process. He asks lots of questions. There's no such thing as too much information—but the trick is knowing what's valuable and what isn't.

Icons

Looking across the collection, some visual shorthand was utilized to represent some of the more universal aspects of process. These iconic artifacts weren't always used in exactly

Silver Cuellar

Jim Haven

David Horridge

Andy Azula

Danny Gregory

David T. Jones

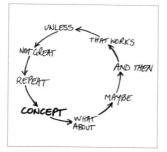

Simon Mainwaring

Deacon Webster

the same ways, but their frequent appearance speaks to their symbolic power.

Circles

ADRIAN ALEXANDER (page 26): The circle signifies a 360-degree perspective, observant from every possible angle.

JANET KESTIN/NANCY VONK (page 103): Concentric circles represent the team and its power to generate many ideas.

SIMON MAINWARING (page 115): Multiple circles combine and create a well-oiled machine: durable and dependable.

Lines and Arrows

DAVID BALDWIN (page 34): The arc linking "idea" and "David" is deceptively simple, given that all of the hard work that separates the two is built into that curve.

HAL CURTIS (page 64): There's something about a dotted line that says, "We're having fun," even when the paths appear so complex and chaotic.

DAVID T. JONES (page 95): Here, the squiggly line captures what it feels like to liberate an idea that was hidden for too long.

KEVIN RODDY (page 134): There's a line for every trick (or ideation technique) in the book and each one of them feels familiar.

Figures

DANNY GREGORY (page 72): The Judge—Although we typically worry about what others will think, sometimes we can be our own worst critic.

MIKE HEID (page 83): The Account Executive—The AE initiates the creative process with the delivery of the brief. Creatives decide whether to view the AE as ally or adversary.

DAVID SWOPE (page 145): The Partner—Speaking of delicate relationships, here's the old ball and chain. Success is based on understanding each other.

The Client—The ultimate arbiter of an idea's viability, qualified to make that evaluation if for no other reason that they're paying for it. (There are great clients and terrible clients out there. Good luck!)

The Client's Spouse—Why does this person's opinion matter? Because the client has to live with this person.

The Focus Group—Is it a good idea to rely upon the opinions of twelve people with nothing else to do? Too many clients think so.

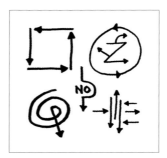

Adrian Alexander

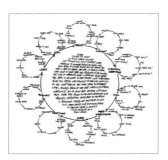

Janet Kestin/Nancy Vonk

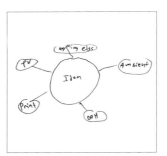

Simon Mainwaring

David Baldwin

Hal Curtis

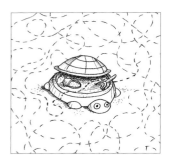

David T. Jones

Kevin Roddy

Danny Gregory

Mike Heid

David Swope

CHAPTER FOUR

Andy Azula

Cal McAllister

Deacon Webster

Mike Heid

David Swope

Chris Adams

Andy Hall

Objects

ANDY AZULA (page 30): Maintain the energy level: Have some (more) pizza. And during that break, enjoy some light reading. Creatives should familiarize themselves with all the work in the award books. It's not there to steal from, it's there to inspire. More pizza?

CAL McALLISTER (page 118): Keep pictures of family and friends around to remember what's really important when the deadline is bearing down. Reserve space on the office book-shelf for favorite sources of inspiration (CDs, DVDs, toys, a PlayStation 3).

DEACON WEBSTER (page 153): It's the breakfast, lunch and dinner of champions—coffee. The hardcore folks take it black. For many writers and art directors, it's fuel.

MIKE HEID (page 83): Appreciate the creative brief for what it's intended to be—a launching pad for even more research and deliberation. The biggest ideas grow from copious amounts of information and insights.

DAVID SWOPE (page 145): Supplemental research will always be part of the job. This is the work that builds upon the brief and fills in any gaps. Each individual develops search strategies and identifies trusted sources that will yield a clearer under-standing of the problem.

Metaphor

It's often easier to communicate to others the true nature of an experience by comparing it to something already familiar or more accessible. In many of the drawings, visual metaphors

Randy Tatum

Andy Azula

are used as a powerful tool for explaining how the creative process feels and unfolds. They enlighten in ways that tran-scend any requisite knowledge of the profession.

The Nature of the Challenge

CHRIS ADAMS (page 22): Creative problem solving requires both skill and artistry, like the cast of a seasoned fly fisherman.

ANDY HALL (page 76): The constant drive to do something different, to discover something new, can feel like swimming against the current.

RANDY TATUM (page 149): In pursuit of the idea, one can feel lost, even trapped. Keep the faith that there's always a way out of the maze.

The Moments of Frustration

ANDY AZULA (page 30): The very human inclination to post-pone dealing directly with the problem at hand can create all kinds of anxiety. Some creatives thrive on it.

Janet Kestin/Nancy Vonk

Ian Cohen

Danny Gregory (a)

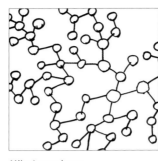

Mike Lescarbeau

Adrian Alexander

David Swope

Kevin Roddy

Danny Gregory (b)

JANET KESTIN/NANCY VONK (page 103): A moment of silence, please, for all the ideas that die along the way. The good news is there's rarely any time to mourn them.

The Incubation Period

IAN COHEN (page 52): Following the initial research, the real work begins. Transform the raw materials—make connections, recognize patterns, develop insights. The true value of research is found in how it's leveraged.

DANNY GREGORY (a) (page 72): Some new ideas are quite fragile. With time, revision and refinement they can become viable. Don't give up on these ideas too soon.

MIKE LESCARBEAU (page 107): Just as the atoms within a molecule create new bonds, an initial idea can be the catalyst for generating many more.

The Discovery of Solutions

ADRIAN ALEXANDER (page 26), DAVID SWOPE (page 145): There's perhaps no more recognizable visual metaphor for an idea. The light bulb signals the "illumination" moment and a product born of the process.

KEVIN RODDY (page 134): Ideas can be discovered many different ways. As we build experience developing them, a cognitive toolbox emerges. The creative process becomes ever more sophisticated and efficient as a result.

DANNY GREGORY (b) (page 72): Patience is a virtue. The end isn't always in sight, but for those who persist and invest in their work, a satisfying outcome is in store.

PROCESS ILLUSTRATED: DIMENSIONS OF THE CREATIVE PROCESS

We've celebrated our contributors' metacognitive expertise and weren't surprised to see their keen understanding of personal creativity manifested in the drawings they submitted. In accepting the challenge to visualize their process (in addition to describing it in words), they offered us a more holistic picture than ever before.

Based on our analysis of this rich data set, we have identified six distinct dimensions of the creative process in advertising. These dimensions help characterize the nature of the process and how it impacts the lives of creative professionals, but we don't identify any new stages or imply any particular sequence of events. We consider these dimensions as a foundation for further study; they are broad strokes, each representing a new area for scholarly inquiry.

We believe most advertising creative directors, art directors and writers will recognize themselves in this work. We hope they'll find this analysis useful as they continue developing their own understanding of how they think and perform. For anyone fascinated by the advertising industry, these dimensions provide more evidence for why it's so compelling. Advertising creativity is, in fact, both an artistic and an intellectual enterprise. And for some of the brightest folks you'll ever meet, it's their passion.

Dimension One: Identity

Who are the creative people that develop advertising's big ideas? Each creative brings a unique perspective to his work,

Advertising creativity is both an artistic and an intellectual enterprise.

of course, but we recognize a few distinct philosophies that are shared among the group profiled in this book. Here, we describe five categories of professional identity and provide some of the best examples of each. These categories aren't mutually exclusive; it's possible for some creatives to fit more than one category. However, we believe most could find a description here that best suits them.

The Explorers

They draw inspiration from everything around them. They're convinced that big ideas come from all the little details. Having a life outside advertising makes for better advertising. Every experience can inform the craft.

Consider:

ANDY AZULA (page 30)
TOM CHRISTMANN (page 49)

The Seekers

They enjoy the hunt. Finding the idea is so challenging and exciting because they appreciate the infinite possibilities. They like to take the search farther and deeper to confirm that they've found the best solution. No stone is left unturned.

Consider:

DUSTIN BALLARD (page 38)
DAVID HORRIDGE (page 87)

The Believers

They marvel at the power of creativity, but they consider it a precious, somewhat fragile phenomenon. Though recognized for their creative expertise, they would rather not over-analyze it and risk compromising it. The process must be protected.

Consider:

DAVID BALDWIN (page 34)
MATTHEW BARBER (page 41)
DAVID KENNEDY (page 99)

The Executors

They have a plan. They are confident in the way they work and they trust the process they've developed over time. This is a function of both experience and success. They've seen it all and taken notes. They feel empowered.

Consider:

DANNY GREGORY (page 72)

RACHEL HOWALD (page 91)
SIMON MAINWARING (page 115)
KEVIN RODDY (page 134)
LUKE SULLIVAN (page 141)
DAVID SWOPE (page 145)

The Collaborators

They are team players. They appreciate the synergy that is created when people with different expertise and perspectives work at the same table. They are considerate of all opinions and want to find solutions that will make everyone proud to be part of the process.

The Explorers

The Seekers

The Believers

The Executors

The Collaborators

Consider:

Dimension Two: Experience

How does experience influence an individual's creative process? Not surprisingly, creatives with more seniority seem to have a clearer understanding of their own process and the professional context in which it operates. They know better than anyone else how tough this kind of work can be, but they also find it extremely rewarding. For that reason, many also feel compelled to help mentor the next generation of idea makers. Here are a few of the lessons that experience seems to teach.

Experience builds confidence: For guys like BBH's Kevin Roddy (pages 134–137), experience is measured by a long and diverse roster of high-profile clients and more creative awards than anyone can count. These days, they don't worry as much about pitching new business; they know the game, and their reputations bring clients knocking. This level of achievement builds confidence in their signature creative approaches and makes them even more valuable to their agencies and clients.

Experience offers perspective: After years of experience, the most important parts of the process become obvious to a seasoned creative professional. For Ross Chowles of the Jupiter Drawing Room (pages 45–48), incubation time is essential to the discovery of a big idea. At 72andSunny, Glenn Cole (pages 56–59) questions everything in order to get to the heart of the problem. Loeffler Ketchum Mountjoy co-founder Jim Mountjoy (pages 122–125) respects the creative brief and leverages the strategic foundation it offers him. Each perspective is drawn from much trial and error and represents a personal key to success.

Experience acknowledges reality: In the pursuit of the idea, there will be bumps along the road, and some solutions will be better than others. Sometimes the process works beautifully, but sometimes it doesn't feel like much of a process at all. As Wieden+Kennedy's Hal Curtis (pages 64–67) observes, there are many constituencies to satisfy and it's tough to make everyone happy with the final creative product—including

yourself. By employing the metaphor of human conception, freelance writer Greg Eiden (pages 68–71) underscores how fragile the process can be. It's impossible to know exactly when or how the idea will be conceived. When it happens, it can feel nothing short of miraculous. As romantic as the notion of creativity can be, the process can be ugly and unpredictable. Experienced creatives know that they must push through the best and worst of times.

Experience promotes sharing: Some of the industry's veteran creative professionals are also powerful mentors. GSD&M's Luke Sullivan (pages 141–144) and mcgarrybowen's Danny Gregory (pages 72–75) are both successful authors whose musings on creativity have enlightened and inspired people everywhere. Fallon McElligott Rice co-founder Nancy Rice (pages 130–133) retired from the agency business and taught at both Miami Ad School and the Minneapolis College of Art and Design, offering the benefit of her experience to aspiring creatives. Renaissance man Simon Mainwaring (pages 115–117) is an active creative director who's also a worldwide speaker on the topics of branding, advertising, creativity and social media. His blog is required reading for anyone plugged in to contemporary practice. Perhaps because someone did the same for them at the start of their careers, these creatives understand the value of sharing what they've learned with others.

Dimension Three: Rhythm

Once the creative process begins, how does the work move forward and get done? It's clear that some creatives like to do their work in a particular order, while others prefer to avoid such patterns. Obstacles to thinking and productivity abound and each individual finds a way to cope with them. And then there's the deadline: The time available to solve the problem is finite. All of these considerations influence the rhythm of the process. Some contributors offered us a sense of how things play out.

Taking It Step by Step

The process unfolds in a series of steps or events. These are generally consistent, regardless of the project. But there's room for adaptation, of course. There's just something comfortable in following a protocol that's tested and true.

Perspective

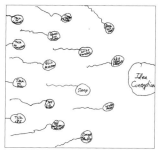

Reality

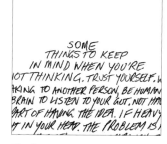

Sharing

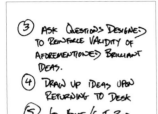

Taking It Step by Step

Waiting, Persisting, Persevering

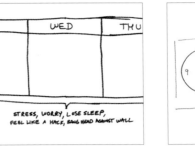

Coping With Fear and Doubt

(Not) Watching the Clock

Large Quantites of Ideas

It's Important to Ask Questions

Consider:

ADRIAN ALEXANDER (page 26)
DANNY GREGORY (page 72)
DEACON WEBSTER (page 153)

Waiting, Persisting, Persevering

The process, although tedious, slow or even stalled at certain points, continues until a solution is found. Clients can't decide, problems are tough or more important projects push this one to next week. This isn't unexpected. In fact, it's the rule rather than the exception.

Consider:

HAL CURTIS (page 64)
ANDY HALL (page 76)
RANDY TATUM (page 149)

Coping With Fear and Doubt

The process can engender fear and self-doubt. Everyone experiences these feelings, but the most effective creatives develop a plan for overcoming them and moving on. Maybe the plan is a technique or simply an inner voice that says, "You can do this."

Consider:

MIKE HEID (page 83)
DOUG PEDERSEN (page 126)

(Not) Watching the Clock

The process is part of a business—the kind with lots of deadlines. Although more than a third of the contributors didn't reference time in their drawings (maybe because it's a given or

maybe because they can't think about it too much), it's always a factor. The goal is to do the best work in the time allotted.

Consider:

RYAN ROMERO (page 138)
JANET KESTIN/NANCY VONK (page 103)
DAVID SWOPE (page 145)

Dimension Four: Values

What are some of the big lessons that our contributors have learned from doing the job? We've articulated five that capture recurring themes from the collection of drawings. They're not listed in order of importance. Most of these statements feel like truths that nearly all creatives would embrace (even the last one, if they're feeling generous).

1. Quality ideas come from large quantities of ideas.

Finding the big idea is like finding the proverbial needle in a haystack. You build the haystack, too.

Consider:

CHRIS ADAMS (page 22)
DUSTIN BALLARD (page 38)
MIKE HEID (page 83)
JANET KESTIN/NANCY VONK (page 103)

2. It's important to ask questions.

Don't take anything at face value. Dig deeper. Challenge the conventional wisdom.

Consider:

ADRIAN ALEXANDER (page 26)
GLENN COLE (page 56)
SIMON MAINWARING (page 115)

3. Creativity is an act of rebellion.

New ideas challenge the status quo. They can make people uncomfortable. They change things. They require bravery.

Consider:

ANDY HALL (page 76)
KATE LUMMUS (page 111)
RYAN ROMERO (page 138)

---

4. A proper work environment is important for creativity.
Create in a place that feels good. The surroundings make a difference. If you don't have a place to be productive, then make one.

Consider:
NANCY RICE (page 130)
DEACON WEBSTER (page 153)

5. Clients don't have to be the enemy.
Clients know their products better than anyone. Bring them into the process. Show that you respect them and they'll respect you. Make them part of the team.

Consider:
JANET KESTIN/NANCY VONK (page 103)

Dimension Five: Rituals

What's our best evidence that the creative process in advertising is much more an art than a science? No creative director, art director or writer does it exactly the same way as another, and that's a very good thing. Rituals are personal, important and fruitful complements to creative thinking. Somehow, they feed the brain so that it can do its best work.

Embrace Your Habits

Creatives engage in a lot of quirky behaviors. But if they serve the process, they're not so quirky. Luke Sullivan (page 141) likes his thumbnail sketches to be a certain size and creates six to eight of them per page. Deacon Webster (page 153) practices drawing the product while he's thinking about it. Ross

Chowles (page 45) uses three personal criteria to choose the best of his ideas.

Break Up the Work With Play

Play is "your reward for thinking so hard," according to Andy Azula (page 30). Whether it's a game of ping-pong, touch football in the park or a little skateboarding, treat that hard-working brain to some fun. Ryan Romero (page 138) recommends catching a matinee or watching some television. "Rot your brain," he advises. "It makes it that much more fertile."

Find Relevance in the Irrelevant

As Greg Eiden (page 68) reminds us, sometimes talking to the dog can be helpful, even if you're not working on a dog food account. Ideas can come from just about anywhere. Mike Heid (page 83) believes in the value of small talk with his art director partner, and Tom Christmann (page 49) pays attention to cab drivers' stories. Don't tune anything out.

Indulge Your Comforts

That's not just any pen, it's Deacon Webster's (page 153) pen of choice, the uni-ball Vision fine tip. Somehow, writing and drawing with that pen feels right. Nancy Rice (page 130) says that listening to classical music helps create the right thinking environment. She prefers a yellow legal pad to an unlined journal.

Pursue Other Passions

David Baldwin (page 34) isn't just a creative director, he's also a guitarist and songwriter in a band. Wieden+Kennedy

Creativity Is an Act of Rebellion

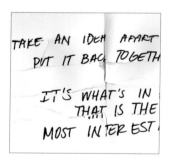

A Proper Work Environment

Clients Don't Have to Be Enemies

Embrace Your Habits

Break Up the Work With Play

Find Relevance in the Irrelevant

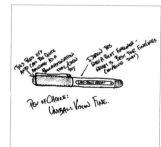

Indulge Your Comforts

Pursue Other Passions

Emotions/Moods/Virtues

co-founder David Kennedy (page 99) works with the American Indian College Fund to support tribal colleges. The best creatives are passionate about advertising, of course, but many find other outlets that offer personal fulfillment.

Dimension Six: Emotions/Moods/Virtues

What's the perspective on life, the attitude, the right mix of personal qualities that helps facilitate success as a creative professional? Many of the answers can be found in the drawings that trace the process. Emotions, moods and good old-fashioned virtues influence the work, and we believe they can also help predict professional success. Most of the top creative people in advertising bring the right mix. Each of the following qualities is followed by a personal affirmation that everyone's little creative voice inside can rehearse and commit to memory.

> **Optimism:** The process is going to be successful if I'm invested in it. I'm capable of solving this problem, which I'll view as an opportunity to do something amazing.

> **Determination:** The process may be fraught with challenges, but I've overcome them before and I will again. Doing so will make me a better creative thinker.

> **Joy/Lightheartedness:** The process should be fun. I'll remember to enjoy it and insist that my colleagues do, too. I'll find the light at the end of all tunnels.

> **Humility:** The process is my own, but it's not about me. I'm lucky to make my living doing something I love. I'm part of a team of people who help me do good work.

CLOSING REMARKS: PROCESS IS IMPORTANT

Now that we've come to the end, let us tell you about the beginning. This project began with a simple "what if?" mumbled late one evening as we looked over some student projects. There were stunning ideas on the table in front of us. We are constantly amazed by what our students can do. They can summon beautiful imagery, use words masterfully and bring it all together as a compelling piece of work. Their perspective is fresh, and finding a different approach is always part of their agenda.

As teachers, we help students channel their individual talents and focus on finding their own creative process. We watch that process grow and mature. By the time they've built a portfolio and are ready to find that first job, a real transformation has taken place. They feel empowered to do the kind of work they've admired in the awards books for years, but to do it even better! The big ideas that inform the world's best advertising set the bar, and the students understand that it's their job to keep raising it.

Then came the "aha" moment. What if all the good work that inspires our students and us could become an even more powerful teaching tool? What if aspiring art directors and writers could learn more about the creation of great work by better understanding the thinking that led to it? What if we could peek inside the brains of some of the best creative pros and see how their ideas are born? The possibilities were exciting.

Like all good ideas, this one became lodged in some wrinkle of our brains and we had to find a way to make it happen. And so this project began. We challenged our colleagues in the business to share their insights and visualize their process. After several years of brainstorming, collaboration, backtracking, organization, production, writing, editing and verifying, it somehow became a book. We imposed upon the good humor and generosity of hundreds of people—our contributors, their assistants, many client reps, (too) many lawyers and maybe a couple of golden retrievers (long story) to collect all the materials you see here. We're convinced that neither of us could have done this alone. One of the co-authors is blessed with a manic obsession for detail and the other works loosely in the big picture world. Creative partnerships thrive on complementary skill sets. We took all possible advantage of this collaboration, then watched as that "aha" moment grew to be this extraordinary (if we do say so) collection.

This project is intended to help bridge the considerable gap between advertising theory and practice. We believe it is relevant to students preparing to enter the field, to the larger community of creatives whose peers are featured here and to anyone who is fascinated by this business. We see potential for this work to inform scholarship, to enrich understanding of the profession and to further legitimize advertising creativity as a powerful cultural force. We also hope that it helps you, the reader, to consider your own identity as a creative thinker. Maybe you'll try doing a drawing yourself.

Ads (even the greatest ones) are just products. Creativity, however, is the human enterprise that brought them into being. It is a rich and wonderful process informed by culture and environment, the straightforward and the serendipitous: your education, your travel to the shoreline or to London or to a new neighborhood, that thing that happened to you in the third grade, the smell of your grandmother's perfume, what you read and watch and subscribe to, where you spend

Saturday nights and Tuesday mornings. As we collected the materials for the book and did the research, we rediscovered that creative thinkers pay attention to it all. They know what stokes the fire, what quirks or rituals or experiences work for them, and they can mentally adapt to tackle a specific problem. This self-awareness helps them power through obstacles and summons that optimistic "it's out there, I just have to find it" outlook. The bottom line: The creative process is personal and nobody does it like you.

Creativity is the stuff that sets mankind apart, the force behind science and art and all human accomplishment. Our objective was to broaden the study of the creative process to include our own discipline—with all its faults—so that both the academic community and those in the advertising profession might better understand it. Academic research and professional relevance are too rarely aligned. This project, using data collected directly from agency ranks and analyzed through the lens of contemporary theories of creativity and metacognition, offers insights we hope both constituencies can find valuable. Historically, this is how the scholarship on creativity has grown; with the addition of new studies that examine how the phenomenon is applied in a variety of different contexts. By presenting research in accessible and relevant terms, we also hope we've advanced the study of creativity by making it understandable and interesting to a larger audience.

The next time you see a great ad, take time to think about the people who developed it. We marvel at their successes every day. Advertising may be about moving goods and services, but it's also about how brands speak within the culture. Creative directors, art directors and writers give them their voice. This book is a testament to both their expertise and their humanity.

Even now, a couple of years and thousands of words down the line, each time we look at the work that's presented here we both discover new insights. It's a delight to dig into this collection and unearth new treasures. We hope that you've made some discoveries of your own and that you'll never see advertising the same way again.

Let's keep thinking about thinking.

RESOURCES

Amabile, Teresa. *Creativity in Context*. Boulder, Colo.: Westview Press, 1996.

Amabile, Teresa. *The Social Psychology of Creativity*. New York: Springer-Verlag, 1983.

Csikszentmihalyi, Mihaly. *Creativity: Flow and the Psychology of Discovery and Invention*. New York: HarperCollins, 1996.

Dewey, John. *How We Think: A Restatement of the Relation of Reflective Thinking to the Educative Process*. Boston: D.C. Heath and Co., 1933.

Flavell, John H. "Metacognition and Cognitive Monitoring: A New Area of Cognitive-Developmental Inquiry," *American Psychologist*, vol. 34, no. 10 (1979): 906–911.

Griffin, W. Glenn. "From Performance to Mastery: Developmental Models of the Creative Process," *The Journal of Advertising*, vol. 37, no. 4 (2008): 95–108.

Guilford, J.P. *The Nature of Human Intelligence*. New York: McGraw-Hill, 1967.

Kover, Arthur J. "Copywriters' Implicit Theories of Communication: An Exploration," *Journal of Consumer Research*, vol. 21, no. 4 (March 1995): 596–611.

Larsen, Steen F. "What Is It Like to Remember? On Phenomenal Qualities of Memory." *Autobiographical Memory: Theoretical and Applied Perspectives*, edited by Charles P. Thompson, Douglas J. Herrmann, Darryl Bruce, J. Don Read, David G. Payne and Michael P. Toglia: 163–190. Mahwah, N.J.: Lawrence Erlbaum Associates, 1998.

Runco, Mark A. and Steven R. Pritzker, eds. *Encyclopedia of Creativity*, vols. I–II. San Diego: Academic Press, 1999.

Sternberg, Robert J., ed. *Handbook of Creativity*. Cambridge: Cambridge University Press, 1999.

Temple, Margaret and Chris McVittie. "Ethical and Practical Issues in Using Visual Methodologies: The Legacy of Research-Originating Visual Products," *Qualitative Research in Psychology*, vol. 2, no. 3 (2005): 227–239.

Wallas, Graham. *The Art of Thought*. New York: Harcourt Brace, 1926.

Young, James Webb. *A Technique for Producing Ideas*. Chicago: Advertising Publications, Inc., 1940.